God Bless
Ed Whyst

Times of Refreshing

Embracing Biblical Repentance

❧❧

ED WRIGHT

CrossBooks™
A Division of LifeWay
1663 Liberty Drive
Bloomington, IN 47403
www.crossbooks.com
Phone: 1-866-879-0502

The cover is an original painting from Jeannie Maddox.

First published by CrossBooks 04/29/2010

ISBN: 978-1-6150-7181-4 (sc)

Library of Congress Control Number: 2010925415

Printed in the United States of America
Bloomington, Indiana

This book is printed on acid-free paper.

*I would like to dedicate this book
to some very special people.*

The first is my wife Jana, who loves me deeply and gives me the security to continue to expand my thinking.

And then there are my two wonderful children.

Haley has been a steady stream that flows from the heart of God.

T has been a wonderful example of the power of repentance.

My parents, Bill and Edith Wright, have taught me lessons of life, lessons that allow me to see God at work.

My in-laws, T. I. and Patsy Long have loved me like their own.

And of course, of primary eminence is my Lord Jesus Christ.

I would to express my great appreciation to Mrs. Jeannie Maddox for allowing me to use her painting for my cover.

Contents

CHAPTER I

Repentance Brings Refreshment

✦

"Repent therefore and return, that your sins may be wiped away, in order that times of refreshing may come from the presence of the Lord (Acts 3:19, NASB).

He knew that like thirsty dogs panting for water, they were panting for spiritual relief for their parched souls.

The lame man—the one born that way, the one who sat at the beautiful gate and begged for food—was putting on a show! He was walking! He was jumping up and down! He was praising God! He was drawing a crowd.

Peter and John had been used by God to heal him. The people ran to the temple in response to the commotion. After all, Jesus had passed that way many times, and this lame man never drew his attention. Was something greater than Jesus at work here?

As the people gathered, Peter began to preach. The first thing Peter did was to tell them that he and John had no power to heal. Peter wanted those listening to know that it was God working through them. It was the power of Jesus.

It did not take Peter long to turn his words toward what he perceived as the crowd's greatest need.

He knew that some of these same people had demanded Jesus's crucifixion.

He knew that some had mocked the Nazarene as he hung on the cross.

He knew that some believed that the miracle on the day of Pentecost was no more than a wild party that had started early and gone bad.

He knew that like thirsty dogs panting for water, they were panting for spiritual relief for their parched souls.

Knowing their condition, Peter—under the leadership of the Holy Spirit—said, "Repent therefore and return, that your sins may be wiped away, in order that times of refreshing may come from the presence of the Lord" (Acts 3:19).

The words of Peter still apply today.

We might be like those who acted in ignorance when they called for Jesus's crucifixion.

We might be like those who looked into the face of spiritual truth only to scoff at its demands.

We might be like those who are still searching for the party gone bad.

We might be like those who finally realize that our souls are parched and the earthly fluids bring no relief.

We might be like those who want so desperately to have our sins wiped away and to experience the times of refreshing which come from the Lord.

Take a look at your heart. God looks there. "God does not see man as man sees man. Man looks at the outward appearance, but God looks at the heart" (I Samuel 16:7). Do you need a time of refreshing? The command of Peter is still true. Repent and return.

What is repentance? Repentance in its simplest meaning is to change one's mind, to change one's direction, or to change one's focus. It is the foundation on which faith must be built.

Satan is powerful and active. His major battlefield is the mind. He is always putting thoughts into our minds that can destroy us. When these thoughts turn into actions, the consequences of our sin become much worse.

Repentance is changing our mind to reflect God's mind. It is sharpening our focus. It is dealing with our sin. It is battling Satan at the site of his greatest strategy. It is gaining victory. It is much more than a thinking process. It is not only changing our minds but changing ourselves.

The apostle Paul wrote much of the New Testament. In his second letter to the Corinthians, he wants to make sure that they understand his previous letter. In First Corinthians, he addresses several severe sins that were occurring in the congregation, and he clearly states God's opinion of those sins. He knew that his frank treatment of those issues would evoke strong emotions. Knowing the possible outcome, he prayed that those emotions would drive the Corinthians to God and not away from him.

He writes, "For though I caused you sorrow by my letter, I do not regret it; though I did regret it. For I see that this letter caused you sorrow though only for a while. I now rejoice, not that you were made sorrowful, but that you were made sorrowful to the point of repentance, for you were made sorrowful according to the will of God, so that you might not suffer loss in anything through us. For the sorrow that is according to the will of God produces repentance without regret, leading to salvation, but the sorrow of the world produces death" (II Corinthians 7:8–10).

Paul knew that when we are confronted with our sin, it is going to produce sorrow. One type of sorrow leads to seeking God's forgiveness. The other sorrow leads to anger and alienation from God. Sorrow is a prelude to choice. The Corinthians would either choose repentance and live or choose anger and die.

Paul is not finished with his teaching. Next he writes these words: "For behold what earnestness this very thing, this godly sorrow has produced in you; what vindication of yourselves, what indignation, what fear, what longing, what zeal, what avenging of wrong! In everything you demonstrated yourselves to be innocent in the matter" (II Corinthians 7:11). In this verse, Paul talks about the things which godly sorrow produces—he mentions seven. As I studied this passage, it seemed to me that the seven things produced by godly sorrow were a progression—starting with an eagerness to be cleansed, and ending with an act of obedience under the leadership of the Holy Spirit. It is that progression that I want us to explore. We will look at each thing produced and see how one builds upon another. Each one prompts us toward true, godly repentance. True, godly repentance leads us to times of refreshing. We will start with an overview and then explore each one in more depth.

EARNESTNESS

Earnestness or *carefulness* is taken from a Greek word that has as a primary meaning *haste* or *speed*. It is an expression of active concern. The first step in repentance is to be actively concerned with our sin. When the Holy Spirit convicts us of our sin, we should speed toward repentance.

This is elementary. Our sin bothers us. But there are times when the Holy Spirit begins to speak to our hearts, and we shut the Holy Spirit out. We shut the Holy Spirit out by procrastination, rationalization, defiance, pride, diversion, etc. If you want the peace that only God can bring, don't shut out the Holy Spirit. Allow the Holy Spirit to convict you of sin, and move quickly toward repentance.

A summary statement that will identify this step is: I am concerned.

VINDICATION OF YOURSELVES

The next step is vindication—an eagerness to be cleared. The Greek word means *to give a speech in defense of oneself.*

Our concern leads to a desire to be cleared. We want to find release from the conviction. We have a desire to get things right. A lot of people who come under the conviction of the Holy Spirit never do anything about it. Some block the conviction; they even fight against it. They wrestle with whether they are going to clear themselves or not. They put their soul on trial. The Greek word for *vindication* is a technical law term. It is used of a person who gives a verbal defense to clear the charges against him. Imagine the Holy Spirit at work. The Holy Spirit argues for God. Satan and his hordes argue the other side. And if the person doesn't listen to the Holy Spirit, their soul will hang in the balance.

If you want to find real peace, real contentment, and not only feel the godly sorrow but have a desire to take it a step further, come to your own defense. Join the Holy Spirit's law team and take a stand against the enemy.

A summary statement that will identify this step is: I want to be cleared.

INDIGNATION

The Greek word means *a feeling of strong opposition or displeasure aroused by something thought to be wrong.* Many people equate indignation with the actions of others, but here it seems to relate to our actions. Here we see our sin as God sees it.

God sees our sin as that which caused the death of his son.

God sees our sin as that which eats away at our fellowship with him.

God sees our sin as that which causes great pain to those he loves.

When we commit sin, our attitude should be one of indignation. We have failed our Master. We have failed our Lord. We are not willing to let this sin defeat us. Finding times of refreshing means we must know our sin disappoints our Lord, and we vow to move past it to victory.

Our response to the moving of the Holy Spirit is not to feel guilty but to experience grief.

We can have victory over our sin!

"But thanks be to God, who gives us the victory through our Lord Jesus Christ" (I Corinthians 15:57).

"For whatever is born of God overcomes the world; and this is the victory that has overcome the world, our faith" (I John 5:4).

"But in all these things we overwhelmingly conquer through Him who loved us" (Romans 8:37).

A summary statement that will identify this step is: I can't believe I would do that.

Fear

The Greek word is the common word used for *fear*. It means *a state of severe stress aroused by intense concern for impending pain, danger, evil, etc.* Some translate it as *alarm*.

As much as we think otherwise, we are weak vessels. We are fallible. It is impossible for us to live the Christian life in our own strength. And when we finally realize that, there is a great sense of fear: fear of sinning again, fear of not being able to keep the commitments made, fear of not being able to enjoy all the blessings that were promised, fear of the punishment of God, fear of being labeled a hypocrite, fear of not having the power to overcome the evil one, fear of coming under God's control, or fear of coming under Satan's control.

I can still remember when I realized that allowing God to control my life produced peace, not fear. As a young man, I thought at times that God got a good deal when he got me. I had some bad points, but basically I was an asset to the kingdom. I was filled with pride. God allowed me to see the results of trying to live a Christian life in my own strength. He allowed me to run on my own energy without his blessing until I used up everything I had. My life was becoming more and more inconsistent. I had the position of a spiritual leader, and I couldn't sense the Holy Spirit.

My private life was less often reflecting the godliness I so desired. I became lonely and depressed. Then finally, lying in a pole vault pit on the campus of Lamar University, looking up into a clear East Texas sky, I realized my need for total dependency on God. I completely surrendered to his care. I had failed, but I was so thankful that he was there to simply say, "I let you get to this point. I love you dearly. You have learned the most basic of lessons. I am God, your creator, your Lord. You are the created. I can help you live a life of victory when you totally depend upon me."

As I have matured in Christ, I realize more and more how much I need him. Our enemy is very strong. He hates God; and therefore, he wants to destroy our lives. I fear Satan's power.

A summary statement that will identify this step is: I am afraid.

LONGING

The Greek word for *longing* means *to long for something; recognizing our lack.*

This is a crucial point in repentance. Too often we have progressed through these steps of repentance—we are concerned, we want to be cleared, we can't believe we did something so stupid and sinful, and we acknowledge our need for help—but then we turn to the wrong person, philosophy, or teachings for help. Instead of longing for God, we settle for man's wisdom.

Sinful people will always try to diminish the severity of sin. They will call it an archaic, Victorian standard and dismiss it. They will call it a moral standard in need of revision. They will try to lessen the accountability. They will try to rule out any spiritual consequences. They will try to bring themselves into a courtroom where the judges are other sinful humans rather than the judge being the Almighty God.

But if you want real peace—if you want real contentment of your soul—long for God, long for his ways, long for his wisdom, long for his touch.

A summary statement that will identify this step is: I long for God.

Zeal

The Greek word for *zeal* means *to have a deep concern for, to be devoted to.*

You can see how this step builds on the previous one. At this point, you are not only longing for God, but you are making a decision to do things God's way. You become devoted to doing those things. This is the motivation before the action.

There have been so many times when we are progressing in repentance and we come to the part where God reveals to us what we need to do—and we say no. We sit in judgment of God. We want the Holy Spirit to speak. But we also listen to what the world has to say. We then retire to our chambers for a judgment. We return and announce to God that we have ruled in favor of our flesh.

Our outcome is the same as King Agrippa when he was listening to Paul's defense in Acts 26. Paul, speaking for God, simply told how he was doing what Jesus had called him to do. He wanted King Agrippa to know that God loved all people. He wanted the king to know that God was making his grace available to both Jews and Gentiles alike. King Agrippa was listening. You could tell by what he said that he was at a point of decision. He said, "In a short time, you persuade me to become a Christian" (Acts 26:28). But as he said this, he ended the conversation and walked out.

He was at the point of release and repentance, but he walked away.

A zealous person doesn't walk away from God. A zealous person embraces God. A zealous person is committed to doing what God says.

A summary statement that will identify this step is: I will do it God's way.

AVENGING OF WRONG

This word translated as *avenger of wrong, or readiness to see justice done,* is the one used here. The word means *to give justice to someone who has been wronged.*

After coming through the whole process, after being concerned, after wanting to be cleared, after dealing with the failure, after being afraid and seeking help, after longing for God, and after having a zeal to do what God wants, one must now go out and do it. The clearing of one's name before the heavenly court is what completes repentance.

John the Baptist told the Pharisees and Sadducees who wanted to come to hear Jesus that they should bring forth fruit in keeping with repentance (Matthew 3:8).

Paul stated that God had given him a mission, and that mission was to declare both to those of Damascus first, and also at Jerusalem and then throughout all the region of Judea, and even to the Gentiles, that they should repent and turn to God, performing deeds appropriate to repentance (Acts 26:20).

What are those deeds?

Although Scripture does not give us a listing of what Paul was talking about, there are some wonderful Scriptures that help us:

1. Confess

"If we confess our sins, He is faithful and just to forgive us our sins and to cleanse us from all unrighteousness (1 John 1:9). The word *confess* is made up of two words—one means *the same* and the other means *word*. It is to speak the same word—to agree with God. We are to agree that what we have done is a sin, and we are to speak that truth when called upon.

2. Restore relationships

"If therefore you are presenting your offering at the altar, and there remember that your brother has something against you, leave your offering there before the altar, and go your way; first be reconciled to your brother, and then come and present your offering" (Matthew 5:23–24). It is so very important to Jesus that before we present a gift in honor of our God, we are right with our fellow men. We must restore any relationships that are broken because of sin.

3. Make restitution

"But if he has wronged you in any way, or owes you anything, charge that to my account" (Philemon 1:18). Here Paul was writing Philemon on behalf of Onesimus. Paul was saying that whatever Onesimus owed by his sinful behavior of running away from Philemon, Paul would take care of it. The Old Testament is filled with references to making restitution for damage done in sinful acts.

Now all these things are from God, who reconciled us to himself through Christ, and gave us the ministry of reconciliation (2 Corinthians 5:18). God has given to us the ministry of reconciliation. Therefore, it seems only right that we should do our best to be reconciled to others.

A summary statement that will identify this last step is: I will restore my name.

Paul brags on the Corinthians because of their response of godly sorrow concerning their sins. He says that they are innocent in this matter. "In everything you demonstrated yourselves to be innocent in the matter" (2 Corinthians 7:11). The word *innocent* here does not deal with their guilt. The word means *pure*. Paul says that they were pure in the way they responded. They did it God's way.

When we repent, times of refreshing will come from the Lord. God spoke through the Apostle Paul to help us understand godly repentance. Each step can be summed up by a short sentence:

I am concerned.

I want to be cleared.

I can't believe that I would do that.

I am afraid.

I long for God.

I will do it God's way.

I will restore my name.

In the next seven chapters we will take a closer look at each step. Please walk with me to the heights of God's redemption.

Remember the words of Habakkuk. He prophesied during a time of great crises. The difficulty of the times did not make him lose his focus. I pray the difficulty of our journey to repentance will not cause us to lose focus either. It will not if Habakkuk's words are a song in our heart.

"Though the fig tree should not blossom, and there be no fruit on the vines, though the yield of the olive should fail, and the fields produce no food, though the flock should be cut off from the fold, and there be no cattle in the stalls, yet I will exult in the Lord, I will rejoice in the God of my salvation. The Lord God is my strength, and He has made my feet like hinds' feet, and makes me walk on my high places (Habakkuk 3:17–19).

CHAPTER 2

Earnestness: I Am Concerned

❧-❦

"For behold what earnestness this very thing, this godly sorrow, has produced in you: what vindication of yourselves, what indignation, what fear, what longing, what zeal, what avenging of wrong! In everything you demonstrated yourselves to be innocent in the matter" (2 Corinthians 7:11).

He lost the kingdom of heaven trying to hold on to a very small piece of the kingdom of earth.

She came into my office. You could tell by looking at her face that she was in a lot of pain. As she told her story, it was evident that she needed a time of refreshing. She talked of the pressures of her life—pressures so great that at times she wanted to kill herself and find the ultimate release. She told me that she was very weary. As we talked, I shared with her the hope we can have in Jesus. I told her that one of the ways people find relief is when they begin to help others. And then it happened. Her squinted brow flattened out. Her stooped shoulders rose upward. Her deeply burdened face broke forth with a smile. She said, "I used to do that!" And for one brief moment, she found relief. She was different. It was as if she put down the heavy load she was carrying. Unfortunately, she returned to her old countenance. But for one moment, she was free.

Many people are held in bondage by the lack of repentance. Times of refreshing can come when we deal with our sin as God teaches us to do.

The Corinthian Christians were a people in transition. They were having a hard time. They had come out of one of the most pagan cultures of their day, and the influences of a rebellious lifestyle were making themselves known in the church. The Corinthians sought holiness, but old attitudes and beliefs lingered. There were fights over which preacher to follow. Was it to be Peter, Paul, Apollos, or Jesus? There was immorality to the point of a son marrying his father's ex-wife. There were many disputes and much talk concerning authority.

Because Paul was greatly instrumental in the birth of the church, he felt an immense responsibility for its growth. So when he heard of the things that were happening there, he wrote them a letter. In that letter were some pointed words. These words were meant to cause godly sorrow. Paul wrote the equivalent of words that had the effect of the scrubbing that takes place before the healing ointment is applied. He knew that his letter would either lead to true repentance or push this rebellious group into further mutiny. There was a risk involved in those words, but Paul was willing to take that risk. He wanted times of refreshing to surge through that church, and he knew that the flow must be driven by repentance. His words were ones that would take the Corinthians to the edge. Would they fall into the arms of Jesus, or would they stumble off the back side of the mountain of anger?

"For though I caused you sorrow by my letter, I do not regret it; though I did regret it—for I see that that letter caused you sorrow, though only for a while—I now rejoice, not that you were made sorrowful, but that you were made sorrowful to the point of repentance; for you were made sorrowful according to the will *of* God, in order that you might not suffer loss in anything through us. For the sorrow that is according to the will of God produces a repentance without regret, leading to salvation; but the sorrow of the world produces death" (II Corinthians 7:8–10).

As scripture so wonderfully reports, the Corinthians were made sorrowful, and they did repent. When the apostle Paul confronted them with their sin, they were greatly concerned. We must be greatly concerned about our sin! Why? Because it affects us in so many ways. As you read through the different results that emerge from sin, ask the Father for his cleansing. If we do not repent of our sin, our very relationship with God is disrupted.

WAYS THAT SIN HINDERS US:

Sin impedes our spiritual progress. "Therefore, since we have so great a cloud of witnesses surrounding us, let us also lay aside every encumbrance, and the sin which so easily entangles us, and let us run with endurance the race that is set before us" (Hebrews 12:1).

Picture in your mind trees with thick underbrush. You can see your brand new Titlist ProV1 golf ball lying under the thorniest bush. As you try to reach it, the briars pull at your shirt, your pants, and your hat. The briars do not want to yield their new treasure. They want to impede the rescuer. Satan guides his hordes of demons to impede us. When we sin, it is as if the clutching thorns grow at an alarming rate. Whenever we find ourselves among the thorns, there is a great possibility that our spiritual progress will be slowed.

Have the thorns of sin pricked your soul to the extent that the pain is hindering your progress?

Sin soils our lives. "But if we walk in the light as He Himself is in the light, we have fellowship with one another, and the blood of Jesus His Son cleanses us from all sin" (1 John 1:7).

There were seven boys in one college house. The small house had been painted and cleaned before they moved in. After a week, you could tell that no one was taking the initiative to keep it clean. A month passed—fraternity parties, trash everywhere. By the end of the semester, it was "enter at your own risk." Doors were busted. Sheetrock caved in. Messages were written all over the walls. Dishes were piled high. Leftovers were growing green and fuzzy. The effects of a take-no-responsibility lifestyle were everywhere. It was a physical example of a spiritual principle. When one displays a take-no-responsibility lifestyle, the resulting sin begins to build. The path to Christ becomes littered. The discarded spiritual food becomes objectionable. There are writings of rebellion all over the walls of the soul. Sin brings filth.

Stop. Smell your life. Is there an odor or a stench? Has sin rotted your heart?

Sin makes us calloused to the moving of the Spirit. "But encourage one another day after day, as long as it is still called "Today," lest any one of you be hardened by the deceitfulness of sin" (Hebrews 3:13).

Picture a lonely, broken-hearted, bitter old woman. She had been lured into a steamy relationship by a smooth-talking, quick-acting Romeo. He promised her new things. He stole her innocence. He left only hated memories. The constant replay of the separation has made her calloused to the wooing of the Holy Spirit. Sin was exhilarating until accountability came. All that is left is a hardened spirit where the steps of regret have walked a million times. Great disappointment is found in many of us. Each time we tread across the fertile soil of our heart, the ground grows harder. The harder it is, the more difficult it is for the things of God to surface.

Have you worn a path through the fruitful garden of God's grace?

Sin results in bondage. "Jesus answered them, 'Truly, truly, I say to you, everyone who commits sin is the slave of sin'" (John 8:34).

"His own iniquities will capture the wicked, and he will be held with the cords of his sin" (Proverbs 5:22).

Same song, second verse—or is it the third verse, the fourth verse, what verse? What makes anyone think that things will be different this time? Being on the other side of the law doesn't seem to matter. Having exposed needle marks all up and down his arm doesn't seem to matter. The absolute disgust of his parents doesn't seem to matter. The thought that he has fought against God one more time doesn't seem to matter. He is a slave to sin.

Is there a temptation that has captured your will?

Sin produces coveting of all kinds. "But sin, taking opportunity through the commandment, produced in me coveting of every kind; for apart from the Law sin is dead" (Romans 7:8).

Picture a young child in the toy store, running joyfully down every aisle, shouting to his parents his desire to own it all. And with every request, a dart hits the heart of mom and dad. They can only get one small toy. Sin wants it all with no regard for the cost. When our minds stray from the will of God, the "I wants" creep in. And it is not long before the "I deserves" find a place of residence. And then the "I must haves" force their way on our mind's screen. The focus is blurred to God's will, and it becomes more focused on our will. When we feed self, it dominates.

Do you care more about your pleasure than God's will?

Sin brings disgrace. "Righteousness exalts a nation, but sin is a disgrace to any people" (Proverbs 14:34).

Picture the woman thrown at the feet of Jesus. She was caught in the very act of adultery. She is being tried in a public arena. Everyone knows the charge. Her mother and father have even been summoned. She hangs her head in shame. The results of sin do not end when the sin is committed.

Has the disgrace of sin driven you away from God and his people?

Sin causes of anxiety. "For I confess my iniquity; I am full of anxiety because of my sin (Psalms 38:18).

Picture an anxious man. How many questions can his mind produce? Will people find out? What will they do when they find out? What will his sin cost him? How can he get out of this? When will he ever be able to rest? Who can deliver him? Hundreds more questions follow. His only reprieve is the pathway to repentance.

Are you more concerned with people finding out about your sin than you are with a restored relationship with Christ?

Sin affects our health. "There is no soundness in my flesh because of Your indignation; there is no health in my bones because of my sin" (Psalms 38:3).

Picture an old cowboy getting out of his battered truck. His body bears the marks of a rebellious life. His family is long gone; his only companion is a bottle. To borrow an old Western saying, "He looks like he was rode hard and put up wet." He coughs profusely in between the puffs on his cigarette. His wild partying has left him a walking invalid.

Our spiritual health is as important as our physical health. How healthy are you?

Sin causes us to waste away. "When I kept silent about my sin, my body wasted away through my groaning all day long" (Psalms 32:3).

Picture a woman screaming at the top of her lungs, "He's hurting me. Help me!" Her screams are disproportionate to what is really happening. She slumps to the floor and becomes lifeless. Her cocaine addiction has taken its toll. She wakes only to scream out a profanity-laced tirade that further reveals the deterioration of her mind.

Has your sin gotten to the point of constant pain?

Sin brings death. "Do you not know that when you present yourselves to someone as slaves for obedience, you are slaves of the one whom you obey, either of sin resulting in death, or of obedience resulting in righteousness?" (Romans 6:16)

"For the wages of sin is death, but the free gift of God is eternal life in Christ Jesus our Lord" (Romans 6:23).

It happened so suddenly! One moment you were praying for a safe return, and the next you open the door and receive a message that tears your heart in two. He is gone. You had prayed and prayed that he would stop drinking. You had spent everything you had for treatment. He had made so many promises. And now there were no more promises to make. You put him in hands of God.

Are you on the brink of death?

Sin impedes our spiritual progress.
Sin soils our lives.
Sin makes us calloused to the moving of the Spirit.
Sin can result in bondage.
Sin produces coveting of all kinds.
Sin brings disgrace.
Sin is a major cause of anxiety.
Sin affects our health.
Sin can cause us to waste away.
Sin brings death.

When we see what sin can do to us, why do we hold on to it?

When God's Holy Spirit comes to convict us, why do we hesitate?

Why aren't we eager to do something about our sin?

Why aren't we earnest in our efforts to cleanse ourselves, find forgiveness, and be refreshed?

Where is the concern?

Are you on the pathway to repentance? Some are not, even though they have been confronted with their sin. They will not travel the path to refreshing. Why not?

Why do people delay?

Complacency and procrastination: Sin is not seen as a real problem. Nothing serious has happened so far.

In a conversation recently, a lady she told me she had breast cancer. She very quickly added that the doctor found it in time. He was able to treat the cancer in its early stages and the chances for reoccurrence were very small. Early detection saved her life.

The results of sin grow like cancer. If they are not dealt with, those results can cause us to die or severely limit what God can accomplish through us.

A man's marriage stood in the balance. Things were not going well. His wife had started going to church, and she wanted him to go with her. As we talked, he acknowledged that God could help. He acknowledged that he needed God. He knew how serious things were. When I left, he was committed to give God a chance. On Sunday afternoon, I called to see how it went. "Well, I didn't go," he replied. "A buddy of mine called and wanted me to go fishing, and I just couldn't say no." In his mind, he thought he still had time to make things right. In my mind, he had just sealed his fate. It wasn't long before he was divorced.

Why do people delay what they know they need to do? God has been speaking to you. He has been convicting you of things that need attention. Some need immediate attention! Are you going to act? Stop right now and confess your sin. Stop right now and repent. Stop right now and make that call or write that letter, text message, or e-mail. Allow the Holy Spirit of God to do his work through you.

Pride: The rich young ruler turned and walked away from one of the greatest invitations of all times. Jesus had invited the ruler to be one of his disciples. He was asked to follow Christ. He was asked to witness the miracles, hear the sermons, grapple with the parables, and receive the explanations. He was asked to sit around the campfires and contemplate the mysteries of the Almighty God. The invitation was to get to know the Savior of the world.

But he refused. Jesus asked him to do one thing. Jesus told the rich man to go and sell everything he had, give it to the poor, and then come and follow him. For the young ruler that was too much to ask. He owned much. He was rich. What about all the hard work, all the shrewd deals, all the recognition, and all his possessions? What would the people think?

"Did you hear about the rich guy? He lost everything he had. Some say he sold it all and gave it to the poor just to follow that Jesus guy. That can't be true. I wonder how he really lost it."

"I heard he squandered it on gambling."

"I heard he got too familiar with the ladies of the evening and one of them took it."

"He sure wasn't a very good businessman."

In his moment of decision, his earthly reputation was more important than his eternal destiny. Maybe he thought he would get another chance, but that never materialized. He lost the kingdom of heaven trying to hold on to a very small piece of the kingdom of earth. Pride can be so devastating.

Defiance: "I'll do what I want. I don't need you or your God." And inside, another layer of defiance covers the heart. Defiance is all about causing pain to others. It's payback time, and the deviant one will use whatever he has that will cause the most pain.

Some people are mad at their parents—especially parents who said one thing and did another, who tried to control and manipulate by guilt, or who used the Bible as a broad sword to inflict pain. When these people perceive pressure, especially pressure to move toward God, they speak words that cut to center of their parent's heart—"Don't come at me with that Jesus stuff."

Anger: "God, it is your fault that I lost the one I loved. She was perfect for me, why did you let that happen?"

"God, it is your fault that my mother died. I needed her. Why did you take her away?"

"God, it is your fault that my business went broke. I worked hard."

"God, it is your fault that I have this disease. How can this happen to me?"

"God, it is your fault that we lost everything in the storm. Why couldn't it have hit somewhere else?"

"God, it is your fault that I didn't make the team."

"God, it is your fault that she received the promotion over me."

"God, it is your fault that I was born this way."

"God didn't do it my way, so why should I do it his way?"

And unless something changes, this person goes off into judgment, shaking their fist at God. We cannot win a fight with God. He is a loving father. He wants us to experience his peace and joy. Our anger will not achieve his blessing. There are so many reasons why things happen. When things happen to you that affect you deeply, instead of blaming God, ask yourself:

"Is it a result of my sin?"

"Is it a result of living in a fallen world?"

"Is it a result of someone else's sin?"

"Is it a result of an accident?"

"What could help me avoid this in the future?"

There is a safety net. There is a wonderful verse that will help us tremendously before the anger builds. "Casting all your anxiety on Him because He cares for you" (1 Peter 5:7).

Rationalization: We rationalize our sin. Ever used one of these?

"My sin is okay because someone made me do it."

"My sin is okay because everyone else is doing it."

"My sin is okay because I saw a Christian doing it."

"My sin is okay because I needed to do it to make me happy, to relieve my pain."

"My sin is okay because it is such a small sin."

"My sin is okay because I wasn't brought up correctly."

"My sin is okay because my parents do it."

"My sin is okay because I haven't had the opportunities that other people have had."

"My sin is okay because I am wealthy and I deserve special treatment."

"My sin is okay because the government really owes me."

"My sin is okay because I am an adult and I can handle it."

"My sin is okay because I should have some credit built from my past righteousness."

There are many examples of rationalization found in the Bible. One of the most pronounced examples is King Saul. In I Samuel 15, the prophet Samuel was sent to King Saul to deliver a message from God. God told King Saul to go and destroy the Amalekites. These were the people that attacked Moses and the people of the Exodus for no reason. At that time, God proclaimed that the Amalekites would pay for this injustice. King Saul was sent to do that. He was told to completely eliminate these people and all their livestock. King Saul went to battle as he was told, but he didn't complete the task. He spared the king and some of the best livestock. When confronted by Samuel, the rationalizations began to pour out.

"But Saul and the people spared Agag and the best of the sheep, the oxen, the fatlings, the lambs, and all that was good, and were not willing to destroy them utterly; but everything despised and worthless, that they utterly destroyed. Then the word of the Lord came to Samuel, saying, 'I regret that I have made Saul king, for he has turned back from following Me, and has not carried out My commands.' And Samuel was distressed and cried out to the Lord all night. And Samuel rose early in the morning to meet Saul; and it was told Samuel, saying, 'Saul came to Carmel, and behold, he set up a monument for himself, then turned and proceeded on down to Gilgal.' And Samuel came to Saul, and Saul said to him, "Blessed are you of the Lord! I have carried out the command of the Lord.' But Samuel said, 'What then is this bleating of the sheep in my ears, and the lowing of the oxen which I hear?' And Saul said, 'They have brought them from the Amalekites, for the people spared the best of the sheep and oxen, to sacrifice to the LORD your God; but the rest we have utterly destroyed'" (I Samuel 15:9–15).

Look closely at verse 15. Here we see rationalization number one: Saul says, "I really don't have any responsibility in this matter. The people did it. Other people interfered with what I wanted to do." Saul makes the same statement in verse 21. The people took some of the spoil. An excuse that is used so often centers around blaming others. "It's not my fault. Others made me do it."

You and I both know that we are responsible for our choices. Others may influence us, but they cannot choose for us. We must take responsibility for our actions. We are bombarded with stimuli which state that we are the victim.

Just the other day I was listening to the advertisements on the radio. This particular one was stating that people's credit card debt was not their fault. It was the credit card companies' fault. They were the ones who made it too hard to pay back what was charged. The ad shifted the blame for the debt away from the one who used the card to the one who issued the card.

That is so like us. We are the ones who commit the sin, but we want to blame it on others who by some means managed to tempt us to sin. Your sin is not someone else's fault.

"Then Samuel said to Saul, 'Wait, and let me tell you what the Lord said to me last night.' And he said to him, 'Speak!' And Samuel said, 'Is it not true, though you were little in your own eyes, you were made the head of the tribes of Israel? And the Lord anointed you king over Israel, and the Lord sent you on a mission, and said, "Go and utterly destroy the sinners, the Amalekites, and fight against them until they are exterminated." Why then did you not obey the voice of the Lord, but rushed upon the spoil and did what was evil in the sight of the Lord?' Then Saul said to Samuel, 'I did obey the voice of the Lord, and went on the mission on which the Lord sent me, and have brought back Agag the king of Amalek, and have utterly destroyed the Amalekites'" (I Samuel 15:16–20).

Look closely at verse 20. Here we see rationalization number two: King Saul thought that just because he did part of what God wanted him to, he did it all. So many of us rationalize our sin by accentuating our obedience. Partial obedience to what God commands us to do does not negate our transgression. We want to redeem our good deeds to cancel out our bad. This is not acceptable to God.

This attitude is prevalent in America. We want to trade Sunday morning church attendance for Saturday night escapades. And if we are super-spiritual and go to church activities twice a week, then that must be worth at least a dozen sins. Our good works will never cancel out our sin.

"But the people took some of the spoil, sheep and oxen, the choicest of the things devoted to destruction, to sacrifice to the Lord your God at Gilgal" (I Samuel 15:21)

Look closely at verse 21. Here we see rationalization number three: Saul did not obey what God told him to do. Instead of destroying everything like he was told, he thought

God would be more pleased by saving some of the spoils and sacrificing them to him in worship. Saul thought he had a better idea than God.

How many times have we said, "I know what God says, but this seems better." We accept the wisdom of man and reject the command of our Lord.

Read the words of this pointed passage of scripture: "There is a way which seems right to a man, but its end is the way of death" (Proverbs 14:12).

"And Samuel said, 'Has the Lord as much delight in burnt offerings and sacrifices as in obeying the voice of the Lord? Behold, to obey is better than sacrifice, and to heed than the fat of rams. For rebellion is as the sin of divination, and insubordination is as iniquity and idolatry. Because you have rejected the word of the Lord, He has also rejected you from being king'" (I Samuel 15:22–23).

God clearly says that our disobedience is called rebellion and insubordination. It is not just an innocent mistake. Our sin is an abomination to our Lord.

"Then Saul said to Samuel, 'I have sinned; I have indeed transgressed the command of the Lord and your words, because I feared the people and listened to their voice'" (I Samuel 15:24).

Look closely in verse 24 and you will see rationalization number four: it is fear. This is one of the most common excuses. "I was afraid of what someone would do to me, so I acted in a way to please them." There are times when our lives are in danger because of the devilish deeds of others. But most of the time, the price we will pay is not life-threatening. When you stand with God, he will stand with you.

"'Now therefore, please pardon my sin and return with me, that I may worship the Lord.' But Samuel said to Saul, 'I will not return with you; for you have rejected the word of the Lord, and the Lord has rejected you from being king over Israel.' And as Samuel turned to go, Saul seized the edge of his robe, and it tore. So Samuel said to him, 'The Lord has torn the kingdom of Israel from you today, and has given it to your neighbor who is better than you. And also the Glory of Israel will not lie or change His mind; for He is not a man that He should change His mind.' Then he said, 'I have sinned; but please honor me now before the elders of my people and before Israel, and go back with me, that I may worship the LORD your God'" (I Samuel 15:25–30).

Look closely at verse 30 and you will find rationalization number five. Saul didn't want to humble himself; he wanted to appear righteous. Here is an excuse that many committed Christians use. "I don't want to confess my sin. I want to act as if it hasn't happened. That way my honor will not be affected. I don't want to discourage others by my sin."

Just in this one incident in the life of King Saul we see him blame his sin on others. We see him rationalize his sin because of the obedient things he had done. We see him substituting what he thought was righteous for what God told him was righteous. We see him use fear to excuse his actions. And we see him even attempt to use his own self-righteousness as a reason not to comply with the wishes of our Lord.

We cannot fool God! There is no excuse that is acceptable to our Lord. Our cleansing comes through our confession.

WHAT ARE SOME BENEFITS OF REPENTANCE?

Repentance offers many benefits. One of the foremost is to escape God's judgment. "I tell you, no, but unless you repent, you will all likewise perish" (Luke 13:3). A terrible atrocity had occurred. Pilate had killed some Galileans and used their blood in a religious ritual. Jesus asked his disciples if they thought that these Galileans were greater sinners than all the other Galileans because of what happened to them. Jesus made a simple point. Unless you repent, you too will suffer judgment. His words imply that unless each person repents, they will suffer judgment no matter what happened to them in their lives. But if one does repent, they will escape.

The Bible speaks plainly about God's judgment, but that message is seldom heard today. The writer of the book of Hebrews wrote, "For if we go on sinning willfully after receiving the knowledge of the truth, there no longer remains a sacrifice for sin, but a terrifying expectation of judgment, and the fury of a fire which will consume the adversaries. Anyone who has set aside the Law of Moses dies without mercy on the testimony of two or three witnesses. How much severer punishment do you think he will deserve who has trampled under foot the son of God, and has regarded as unclean the blood of the covenant by which he was sanctified, and has insulted the Spirit of Grace? For we know Him who said, 'Vengeance is mine, I will repay.' And again, 'The Lord will judge His people.' It is a terrifying thing to fall into the hands of the living God." (Hebrews 10:26–31). Please repent. Please come to the Lord God Almighty and seek his face.

Repentance leads the way to God. How many times have we come back to the ways of God only to face severe obstacles? The way to the Lord is filled with barriers. Repentance helps clear away the impediments we have caused by our sin. Ezekiel writes, "'Therefore I will judge you, O house of Israel, each according to his conduct.' Declares the Lord God, 'Repent and turn away from all your transgressions so that iniquity may not became a stumbling block to you'" (Ezekiel 18:30).

Our way to God is often blocked by:

The rocks of our rebellion,
The sinkholes of our selfishness,
The faults of our fear,
The ditches of our disobedience,
The mudslides of our maliciousness,
And the potholes of our pride and procrastination.

Repentance can clear the way. Why travel a dangerous path instead of a protected path? Why not repent?

Another benefit of repentance is to be spiritually refreshed. "Therefore repent and return, so that your sins may be wiped away, in order that times of refreshing may come from the presence of the Lord" (Acts 3:19).

Are you weary?

How many more times can you express your anger at God because he is not giving you what you desire?

How many more times can you repress the bitterness when someone disappoints you?

How many more times can you stare into nothingness as you consider your hopelessness?

How may more times can you live with the effects of sexual passion and the grime that accompanies it?

God offers a time of refreshing! He offers cleansing. He offers the robes of righteousness. He offers the fragrance of purity. Repent and times of refreshing will come from the Lord.

Repentance also leads to life. "And when they heard this, they quieted down, and glorified God, saying, 'Well then, God has granted to the Gentiles also the repentance that leads to life'" (Acts 11:18). Living in rebellion against God is like walking the earth as a modern-day zombie. You are physically alive, but something has died inside.

Your heart pumps, but it doesn't help you pray.

Your brain responds to stimuli, but it does not respond to the Spirit.

Your lungs help you breath, but they do not help you believe.

You are walking death.

Repentance infuses you with God's medicine for the soul and gives you life. You can take the treatment God has prescribed for you and find a spiritual life that you never knew existed. Which will it be—life or death?

We all know that sin has consequences. And one of those consequences is loss. "I now rejoice, not that you were made sorrowful, but that you were made sorrowful to the point of repentance; for you were made sorrowful according to the will of God, so that you might not suffer loss in anything through us" (II Corinthians 7:9). Sin steals. We lose. There are many losses, such as the loss of innocence, the loss of uninhibited joy, the loss of trust, the loss of purity, the loss of relationships, and even the loss of life.

Repentance is spiritual CPR. Repentance does not provide cardiopulmonary resuscitation, but it does provide a Christian Person's Revitalization.

Sin steals away our joy, kills the benefits of holiness, and destroys the channel of God's love. Shouldn't we be earnest and eager to remove its influence from us? Shouldn't we run to God to repent?

Shouldn't we be concerned?

CHAPTER 3

Vindication: I Want to Be Cleared

✦✦

"For behold what earnestness this very thing, this godly sorrow, has produced in you: what vindication of yourselves, what indignation, what fear, what longing, what zeal, what avenging of wrong! In everything you demonstrated yourselves to be innocent in the matter" (II Corinthians 7:11).

And instead of believing the testimony of the Most High, we believe in the trickery of the Most Low.

rugs had been a great part of his life. It had gotten to the point where even his mother and father were letting the natural consequences occur. Once again, he picked up the phone on the other side of the glass and expressed his desire to change. "I don't want to do this anymore. I don't want to steal from those whom I love just to support my habit. I don't want to be here in this jail. I don't want to disappoint anyone anymore. What can I do?"

There was no doubt that he had passed the "I am concerned" stage. He knew his sin and the high cost of continuing. He was in a place where there was the possibility of his deliverance, and he wanted to travel the road to the times of refreshing.

Was it forced? Was it genuine? Would the desire be enough? Those questions will be answered in the future, but the first step is expressing the desire to be cleared.

Vindication: I Want to Be Cleared

The second step of godly sorrow which leads to repentance comes from a Greek word that is translated, *eagerness to clear yourself*. It is a word that literally means *a speech given in defense of one's self*. If you give a speech to defend yourself before the Almighty judge, it would be well served to know what the judge favors. This step has to do with knowing God's will and becoming committed to it. It is moving from inspiration to implementation.

Our concern leads to a desire to be cleared. We want to be released from the conviction. We have a desire to do the right thing. A lot of people who come under the conviction of the Holy Spirit never do anything about it. They don't block the conviction; they fight it. They wrestle with whether they are going to clear themselves or not. They put their soul on trial. The Greek word used here is a technical law term. It is used to mean *a person who gives a verbal defense to clear the charges against them.* Imagine the Holy Spirit at work. The Spirit argues for God, and Satan argues the other side. The judge calls for you, the plaintiff, to state why you should be cleared of the charges. You stand before the Judge and begin to speak. His penetrating eyes evaluate the honesty of your every word. It is time to speak the truth.

Even at this point, there are those who want to play games with God. They believe that he is unable to judge the thoughts and intentions of the heart. And so they try to present ways to skirt real honesty. It will not work; it never does.

Ways to be dishonest in our attempt to be honest

Are you hiding under the mantle of God's grace? This is a person who does not put a lot of thought or energy in how to avoid sin. This person doesn't seek to do things that help them abstain from sinning. They have a very lackadaisical attitude about their life. If they sin, they can just call for grace. They get on the prayer line and dial God. "God, I need a little grace right now. I expect instant delivery." God's grace is wonderful. It is magnificent! But it is not like some coin-operated machine where you can deposit a prayer and out pops instant grace. God looks at your heart. God wants you to understand the cost. God wants your motivation to be the restoration of a broken relationship, not medication for a bruised conscience.

The audacity of this couple was hard to accept. The couple consisted of a man separated from his wife and a single woman. The man had left his wife and his fifteen-year-old son for his new love. This single woman was to inherit a large sum of money. The separated man turned his back on his wife of many years to embrace his new money—I mean, his new love. They were seen together even before the divorce proceedings had started. They had no regard for how the man's ex-wife and son felt. When his ex-wife protested, the new couple sent her a tape called *Letting Go of Your Past.* It was from one of the leading preachers of a grace-oriented ministry. This new couple wanted the ex-wife just to ignore their sinful life style and accept God's grace like they had. After all, God saw the love between them, and even though they were living in sin, it was all right.

Are there things that you are doing that are in direct violation of God's word? Do you continue doing them because you can cover them up with grace? Grace is not a substitute for obedience. Grace is the safety net to help us continue our quest for obedience.

Are you forgetting about your sin and acting as if nothing happened? Forgetting represses. Forgiving releases. If we just forget about the times we have sinned against someone or the times they have sinned against us, we only push those feelings under the surface. The issues are not resolved. That incident enters into our memory bank. We store those accounts. One day, under stressful circumstances, all our suppressed emotions come out. It is like we emotionally vomit.

Forgiveness releases. If someone asks you to forgive them and you tell them that you will, you have just deleted the file. You are placing that act in the hands of God. You are employing our Savior as your counselor when it comes to dealing with the manipulative provocations of Satan. We know that Satan will try to have us remember the sinful acts time after time. But when he starts his attack, we call for our counselor. We tell Satan that Jesus in handling that case! Forgetting our sin and not achieving forgiveness is like depositing worthless stock into your retirement account thinking that the bank will not know the difference.

The weeping was almost uncontrollable. It was very difficult to understand what he was saying in between his gasping for breath. Before me was a man in his early twenties that had reached a crisis point in his life. A highly desired relationship had caved in. And it wasn't the first time. The woman he had been with was supposed to be his way to stability. She was supposed to supply the love that he had so desperately needed. She was the one who would help him forget all the tragedies of the past. As he continued to spew forth the emotional bile, he made a statement that revealed much about the cause of his devastation. "I just wish I could go on and be with Jesus. I have been messed up since I was thirteen years old. It's the same thing. I am so tired." Between the lines, you could hear the unresolved issues that had lingered for over ten years. There were things in his past that he had not dealt with that had been suppressed for so long but were finally beginning to surface.

If you think that you can just forget about your sin and that it will not affect anyone, then you are mistaken. When we have a true desire to clear ourselves, we must seek forgiveness. Forgetting is a time bomb.

Are you trying to work your way back into someone's favor? True repentance is not admitting your sin and then inventing a detailed plan to work your way back into someone's favor. It is not giving the person gifts to take the place of personal interaction. The greatest gift you can give someone is to show them that you care deeply when there is a rift in your relationship and that you will take whatever steps are necessary to mend it.

Your loved one wants to look into your eyes, not look into a Hallmark card.

Your loved one wants to hold your hand, not hold the coldness of plastic or metal.

Your loved one wants to see genuine concern, not the quality of the garment by reading the label.

Your loved one wants to hear your voice, not some other voice that can be transmitted over myriads of electronic devices.

Your loved one wants you, not a substitute.

She was taken so young. An automobile accident at age fifteen had claimed her life. As I sat with her mother and siblings in the hospital room, her estranged father arrived. He acknowledged our presence but went straight to his daughter's side. For the next ten to fifteen minutes, he whispered in his dead daughter's ear. As I observed his actions, I thought, "It's a little late." There had been abuse in this family. Her parent's divorce happened years ago. The communication between father and daughter was almost nothing.

He could not work his way back into his daughter's good graces, because it was too late. We cannot work our way back into God's good graces. He doesn't want our self-determined actions. He wants our humble devotion. Instead of wanting to be cleared of our sin, many want to be paid in forgiveness. Many think that they have put enough effort into it, so they deserve forgiveness. God's word says that our good works are as filthy rags.

Good works are never an alternate for godly obedience.

Is saying "I'm sorry" enough? There are a lot of reasons to be sorry.

You can be sorry that you were caught. The crying comes, and the seemingly repentant heart surfaces. But the minute the threat of reprisal is taken away or diminished to the point where the one who is sorry is able to dismiss it, the "I'm sorry" is usually changed into "I'll see you."

You can be sorry that you are experiencing pain. Most people do not like to cause pain to another human being. So when a person sees that they have hurt someone else, the "I'm sorry" lasts as long as the other person is demonstrating pronounced pain. As soon as the expression of pain is gone, the "I'm sorry" turns into "I hope you will be all right."

You can be sorry that you must suffer consequences for your actions. Our sin usually costs us something. The "I'm sorry" usually lasts as long as the restitution. When the emotional or material restitution is complete, then the "I'm sorry" turns into "Get over it."

Verbally saying "I'm sorry" without true repentance is like saying "I love you—as long as you meet my needs." Both are very conditional. The path to times of refreshing is blocked by conditional beliefs, but cleared by humble obedience.

Are you limiting your confession of remorse only to those who are most important to you and leaving others out? It was an accident. Kids were playing, and something was broken. It happened at school, so the vice principal was called. The young man who broke the piece of equipment began to squirm his way out of trouble. Yes, he would tell his parents. Yes, he would pay for the damage. Yes, he was sorry and would do everything he could to take care of the matter quickly. However, it turned out there were a few problems. He gave the principal the wrong contact number for his parents. When there was no payment for the broken item, he told his fellow student that the check was in the mail. He was taking care of it, all right—but he was doing it in an ungodly way. As a matter of fact, he never told his parents. They found out three weeks later when the vice principal finally found the right phone number. When the real story came out, he was sorry again. He was sorry that he lied to the vice principal. He was sorry that he lied to his classmate about the check. He was very sorry that he never told his parents. To restore the situation would take more than a repentant heart before his parents. They were the ones he was most concerned about. Surely if he fixed things with them, then the rest would fade away into insignificance. Much to his dismay, true repentance meant a trip to the vice principal's office for a conference. Next there was the restoration of his relationship with his classmate. Then he had to address his friend's parents who were waiting for a payment to repair or replace the equipment.

Everyone affected is important to God and must be addressed if times of refreshing are to come.

God is the judge. He determines whether we will be allowed to continue our quest for true repentance. He is the one who will propose the plan for our restoration. He is the one who knows us more than we know ourselves and will help us do exactly what we need to do to be restored. And when he reveals his will, there are some who will not act upon it. Why not?

WHAT KEEPS US FROM DOING THINGS GOD'S WAY?

The task seems too big. Do remember the story of Gideon? Read the following verses:

"Then the angel of the Lord came and sat under the oak that was in Ophrah, which belonged to Joash the Abiezrite as his son Gideon was beating out wheat in the wine press in order to save it from the Midianites. And the angel of the Lord appeared to him and said to him, 'The Lord is with you, O valiant warrior.' Then Gideon said to him, 'O my lord, if the Lord is with us, why then has all this happened to us? And where are all His miracles which our fathers told us about, saying, "Did not the Lord bring us up from Egypt?" But now the Lord has abandoned us and given us into the hand of Midian.' And the Lord looked at him and said, 'Go in this your strength and deliver Israel from the hand of Midian. Have I not sent you?' And he said to Him, 'O Lord, how shall I deliver Israel? Behold, my family is the least in Manasseh, and I am the youngest in my father's house.' But the Lord said to him, 'Surely I will be with you, and you shall defeat Midian as one man'" (Judges 6:11–16).

God called Gideon to deliver his nation from their enemy, the Midianites. Of course, Gideon began to give excuses for why he could not do it. You can imagine what was going through his mind. "Now come on, God. Here I am, beating out this grain in a hole so no one will see me, because I am extremely afraid of the Midianites—and you want me to deliver Israel? You have the wrong person."

Some people are asking, "God, you want me to do what? You want me to seek to live an obedient life? You want me to restore relationships? You want me to walk humbly even when I have been wronged? You want me to go to them and ask forgiveness? The task is much too large. You have the wrong person."

How did God help Gideon? Look at the angel's greeting in verse 12: "The Lord is with you, O valiant warrior." God saw in Gideon what Gideon could not see in himself. God sees in us far more than we see in ourselves. Remember that we are going in the name of the Lord Jesus Christ. We are going to bring honor to him. He requires that we be faithful, not that we be successful in the eyes of others. Even if the person we approach is not responsive to our sincere desire to get things right, we have not failed. With God, our obedience is more important than the results. We are to obey. He is the one in control of the results. Go forward, "O valiant warrior!"

We see ourselves as unworthy. God comes to us with a high calling. We are to be his messengers. We are to be the ones who are doing things in a godly way. And just when we have ourselves convinced that we can do it, Satan approaches and plays one of his favorite songs—"You ain't nothing but a hound dog." And instead of believing the testimony of the Most High, we believe in the trickery of the Most Low.

King Saul saw himself as unworthy.

"When Samuel saw Saul, the Lord said to him, 'Behold, the man of whom I spoke to you! This one shall rule over My people.' Then Saul approached Samuel in the gate, and said, 'Please tell me where the seer's house is.' And Samuel answered Saul and said, 'I am the seer. Go up before me to the high place, for you shall eat with me today; and in the morning I will let you go, and will tell you all that is on your mind. And as for your donkeys which were lost three days ago, do not set your mind on them, for they have been found. And for whom is all that is desirable in Israel? Is it not for you and for all your father's household?' And Saul answered and said, 'Am I not a Benjamite, of the smallest of the tribes of Israel, and my family the least of all the families of the tribe of Benjamin? Why then do you speak to me in this way?'" (I Samuel 9:17–21).

Samuel approached Saul because of the word of the Lord. He was to anoint Saul as the first king of Israel. Saul couldn't believe that. He was from the least of all the tribes. He didn't have the bloodline. He wasn't one who was supposed to be chosen. How could he lead the people of the Almighty?

When God calls us to do a task for him, when he calls us to be a peacemaker, when he wants us to live the gospel in front of others, Satan makes sure that we are bombarded with the fiery arrows of unworthiness. The truth is that we are unworthy! We are unworthy to be the messenger of the

Almighty. But our worth comes from Jehovah. He created us. He charted our paths. He gifted us for his service. He believes in us.

Saul failed as the first king of Israel because he tried to take things into his own hands. Instead of staying humble, he began to take on roles that were not intended for him. He wanted to expand his influence even to the point of taking the place of the priests. He compensated for his feelings of unworthiness by seeking to control.

God knows our heart. The next king was David. God told Samuel to go anoint one of Jesse's sons. He looked at those who were present and was immediately captured by Eliab. Eliab looked the part.

God responded, "Do not look at his appearance or at the height of his stature, because I have rejected him; for God sees not as man sees, for man looks at the outward appearance, but the Lord looks at the heart" (1 Samuel 16:7).

When you are inspired to make spiritual changes in your lives, don't worry that you are unworthy. Don't think that you are the least. Know that God looks at your heart. If your heart desires God, then act. Yield yourself to God. There is no one who is outside the love and power of God.

It appears too easy. This excuse was made in a very pointed way by Naaman.

"Now Naaman, captain of the army of the king of Aram, was a great man with his master, and highly respected, because by him the Lord had given victory to Aram. The man was also a valiant warrior, but he was a leper" (II Kings 5:1).

Naaman was told that there was a great prophet in Samaria who could heal his leprosy. So the king of Aram sent a letter to the king of Israel saying that he was sending his great captain Naaman there to be healed. The king of Israel lost control. He couldn't heal anyone. The king thought that his rival, the king of Aram, had sent that message to him to start a quarrel.

Fortunately for the king of Israel, Elisha heard of the king's dilemma and told him to send Naaman to him.

"So Naaman came with his horses and his chariots, and stood at the doorway of the house of Elisha. And Elisha sent a messenger to him, saying, 'Go and wash in the Jordan seven times, and your flesh shall be restored to you and you shall be clean.' But Naaman was furious and went away and said, 'Behold, I thought, "He will surely come out to me, and stand and call on the name of the Lord his God, and wave his hand over the place, and cure the leper." Are not Abanah and Pharpar, the rivers of Damascus, better than all the waters of Israel? Could I not wash in them and be clean?' So he turned and went away in a rage. Then his servants came near and spoke to him and said, 'My father, had the prophet told you to do some great thing, would you not have done it? How much more then, when he says to you, "Wash, and be clean"?' So he went down and dipped himself seven times in the Jordan, according to the word of the man of God; and his flesh was restored like the flesh of a little child, and he was clean" (II Kings 5:9–14).

Some of us respond like Naaman. "I came all the way to God, and he wants me to do what? He wants me to repent? That's all? My sin is far too debilitating! How can he refresh my heart through simple faith? There must be a catch."

So instead of traveling down the path of peace to find release, we store our sins because we think that they are not worth dealing with. In the storage compartment of our heart, the sin eats away our soul as leprosy does a human body.

Do you want to be cleared? If the answer is a sincere yes, then listen to the voice of God and act. Don't waste time making excuses. Do it God's way. Press on to continue the journey to times of refreshing.

CHAPTER 4

Indignation: I Can't Believe I Would Do That

❖

"For behold what earnestness this very thing, this godly sorrow, has produced in you: what vindication of yourselves, what indignation, what fear, what longing, what zeal, what avenging of wrong! In everything you demonstrated yourselves to be innocent in the matter" (11 Corinthians 7:11).

We must not hurry on so quickly that the spill from our sin is just whipped away by one smooth stroke of God's grace.

I don't often meet a man like him, a community leader who is also a church leader. He came to me for counseling on the recommendation of one of our church members. Apprehensively he began to tell his story. He had been unfaithful to his wife. The only people he had told were his wife and his father. Everyone regarded him with high esteem. People in the church continued to seek his guidance. People in the community requested his wisdom. They all looked to him as a model.

He told me about the battle he was having inside. And then he began to weep. He said he was so tired of having people look to him. His sin was bearing the fruit of misery. But this was the refreshing part. He wasn't blaming anyone else. He didn't make excuses. His desire was to follow the path of true repentance. He didn't want a quick fix. He didn't want someone to quote I John 1:9 to him ("If we confess our sins, He is faithful and righteous to forgive us our sins and to cleanse us from all unrighteousness.") and tell him to forget about it. He wanted renewal. He wanted accountability. He wanted a changed heart.

In the first two chapters, we dealt with the intellectual aspect of repentance. We are earnest, eager to find repentance because of the effects of sin upon our lives. We seek to stand before the Almighty God and find forgiveness, but we must know what he wants us to do and not do. We seek to discover the truths of how to obtain times of refreshing.

But Paul teaches us that the path to repentance not only has an intellectual element but it also has an emotional element. The next three characteristics of godly sorrow have an emotional bent.

INDIGNATION: I CAN'T BELIEVE I WOULD DO THAT

The word *indignation* means *a feeling of strong opposition and displeasure aroused by something wrong.* Have you ever committed a sin and then been very disgusted at your action? You have even cried out, "I can't believe that I would do something like that!"

The party was rocking with no parents in sight. Everything was going according to plan. He didn't think all the cars outside would be the cause of neighborly suspicion. The noise wasn't really that loud, was it? After all, they were inside. It never crossed his mind that his parents didn't have a reputation as party people. Who would ever know?

Two days later, he sat on the couch with his head in his hands. His parents had confronted him. He lied at first, but with probing question after probing question, he finally came to the end of all the excuses he had prepared. Then, with the realization of what happened and what could have happened, he confessed, "I'm an idiot. I can't believe I let you down like this. I can't believe that I would do something against all that you have taught me. I just don't understand how I could do something like this."

People have a love affair with pleasure and ease. Most things invented are for our comfort. When I look back on the things that have been invented in my lifetime, I am amazed. The list includes: microwave ovens, computers, video recorders, video cameras, CD players, DVD players, cell phones, digital cameras, high-definition televisions, the internet, etc. We like comfort, and that comfort has crept into our Christianity as well—especially in dealing with our sin. We want to confess and receive immediate relief without concerning ourselves with the consequences of our actions.

Paul is saying that there must be an interlude, an interruption, a break on the journey from sin to grace. We must not hurry on so quickly that the spill from our sin is quickly wiped away by one smooth stroke of God's grace.

How did Peter handle his failure? Do you remember the incident of Peter denying he was a follower of Jesus? He had boldly boasted that even if he had to die for Jesus, he would never deny him. Jesus knew what was before him. He knew what he had to face and what Peter would face. He knew Peter would fail, and he told him so. "Before the rooster crows, you will deny me three times."

"There is no way I will do that," Peter thought.

One thing you can say for Peter is that he followed Jesus into the arena of confrontation. He was there while they were questioning Jesus. At first, he might have been ready to fight. Did he still have his sword? But as he listened to how condemningly they accused Jesus of blasphemy, he began to weaken. The first denial came at the hands of a servant girl. "You are not also one of this man's disciples, are you?" He said, "I am not." The second came as the spectators warmed themselves around a fire. They said to him, "You are not also one of his disciples, are you?" He denied it, and said, "I am not." And lastly, the challenge came from one who probably witnessed his boldness in the garden. One of the slaves of the high priest, being a relative of the one whose ear Peter cut off, said, "Did I not see you in the garden with Jesus?" Peter denied it again. And this time Luke reports that he cursed. John says that Jesus looked at him. And then the rooster crowed. (Luke 22:54–62)

What was Peter's response? He went out and wept bitterly. He was filled with remorse. He was filled with indignation. The weight of the sin drove the spike of remorse deep within his soul. That would be a night that he would never forget.

What would a twenty-first century response from Peter look like? Would the New Testament been written differently if Peter would have responded like this: "Okay, I did something wrong. It's not a big deal. I was under pressure. I was just protecting myself. After all, I know a lot about Jesus. All that would be lost. Jesus himself said, 'Don't let your heart be troubled and don't let it be afraid.' I certainly was becoming uncomfortable and afraid. I had to get out of there. Don't blame me. Blame John. He is the one who talked the doorman into letting me in. It's all his fault. My being Jesus's disciple was getting very serious. I could have been next on their list. Surely God didn't want me to suffer."

Peter made no excuses. He wept. He was indignant. He couldn't believe that he would do something like that.

There is a great danger here. Make sure that you do not blame God. Make sure you are disgusted with yourself and not God.

I had been meeting with a man for several weeks who was searching for some peace in his life. His anger had cost him his job. But for the last several months, he had put forth an extreme effort to be faithful to what he thought God wanted him to do. His quiet time was well regimented. He recorded his prayers to see what God was doing. The Bible became his textbook. He led his family to be faithful in church. He was making great deposits into God's bank of obedience, and it was time for the withdrawal. It was time for God to do his part. Sure, he had sinned, but after four and a half months, certainly his deposits covered his debt. The only problem was that God had not given him a good return on his investment. God had not restored him to his profession. God had not made sure that he would not have to move but that he would find a new position in the same city. God just didn't care.

So for an hour and a half we talked through his thinking process. He readily admitted his sin. He was angrier with himself than he was with God. But part of his anger was directed at what he saw as injustice. Surely he should get credit for all of his recent efforts. Why wouldn't God even acknowledge all the good deeds he had done? God just didn't care. Since God didn't care about him or his family, he really didn't know whether he could be a follower of God any longer.

This man became indignant, all right. But his indignant attitude was being equally directed at himself and at God. Because of that, there would be no peace. There could be no time of refreshing.

Transferring our anger away from ourselves to God has been something that has been going on for a long time. We must not confront God; we must conform to God.

How did Moses handle his anger? Moses had a bout with being angry at God. Let's investigate:

"Now Moses heard the people weeping throughout their families, each man at the doorway of his tent; and the anger of the Lord was kindled greatly, and Moses was displeased. So Moses said to the Lord, 'Why hast Thou been so hard on Thy servant? And why have I not found favor in Thy sight, that Thou hast laid the burden of all this people on me? Was it I who conceived all this people? Was it I who brought them forth, that Thou shouldest say to me, "Carry them in your bosom as a nurse carries a nursing infant, to the land which Thou didst swear to their fathers"? Where am I to get meat to give to all this people? For they weep before me, saying, "Give us meat that we may eat!" I alone am not able to carry all this people, because it is too burdensome for me. So if Thou art going to deal thus with me, please kill me at once, if I have found favor in Thy sight, and do not let me see my wretchedness'" (Numbers 11:10–15).

The people of the exodus were complaining again. This time it was about the menu. They were tired of baked manna, fried manna, broiled manna, grilled manna, or blackened manna. They remembered the fresh vegetables, the delicious watermelons, and the succulent flavoring from the leeks, the onions, and the garlic. They wanted no more manna. And on top of all of that, they were standing at the doors of their tents, trading one disparaging remark after another.

Moses, the great leader, got mad. He had quickly forgotten all that God has done to bring his people out of Egypt. His faith had been taken captive by his anger.

In verse 11, Moses asked God why he was so hard on him. The word for *hard* carries with it the idea of doing evil. Moses thought that God has done him evil. Moses' sin of faithlessness had now given birth to an attack on the very character of God. And if we do not focus our indignation on ourselves, it can easily lead us to accusing God of doing evil things to us.

In verse 11, Moses also stated that he was mad at God because God had placed a burden on him. The word *burden* reflects the burden carried by a donkey. Sometimes we feel as if God has placed a burden on us. We get tired. Then when we sin in response to our perceived burden, we blame it on God. It's God's fault, because he made us so tired. If the burden was lighter, we would not have buckled under it.

In verse 12, Moses was mad at God because he gave Moses responsibility for all his people. Moses told God that he certainly didn't plan the births of all the people. He was tired of hearing them complain. He was tired of trying to get them to look toward the land of their freedom rather than back toward the land of their captivity. Sometimes we get mad at God because of where he puts us. We are around people we do not like, and that causes us constant irritation. So if we sin, it is God's fault. He should have put us around better people.

Again in verse 12, Moses expressed anger at God because he thought that God wanted him to carry these people to the Promised Land as a father would a baby. Carrying the baby was not the problem. Putting up with a baby and acting like a baby was. Sometimes we get mad at God because he brings circumstances in our lives that are beneath us. We are too good to deal with common problems. If we sin, it is because we shouldn't be dealing with this in the first place. We deserve better.

Then in verse 13, Moses uttered another reason to be mad at God. He had no way of providing meat for all the people. He asks, "Where am I going to get meat to feed all of them?" Sometimes we get mad at God because adults do not act like adults. They act like children and provoke us to sin. If they are going to act like children, then we are justified in treating them like children.

Moses was mad. He was mad at God. If he would have been mad at himself for not having faith in God and then sought God's forgiveness and his will, Moses would have pleased the Father. Let's direct our anger at our failures and not blame God. He is our source of forgiveness. He is our source of restoration. He is our source of times of refreshing.

What about our rights? If Satan can get us to focus on our sin being God's fault, he has, in effect, stopped the process of repentance and therefore stopped us from our receiving times of refreshing. We often place before God our bill of rights. If God does not deliver, then the problem is with him and not with us.

We think as Christians we have the right to good health. And when there is sickness, we can easily sin by allowing our pain to numb us to God's care.

We think as Christians we have the right to be wealthy. And when there are financial struggles, we can sin by demanding God deliver on our timetable.

We think as Christians we have the right to prosper at whatever we do. And when the road turns difficult and the path is covered with mud, we often sin by putting ourselves before God.

We think as Christians we have the right to emotional stability. And when the doubts come, when the anger rages, or when the temptations are ever-present, we sin by defining God's presence as the absence of angst.

We think as Christians we have the right to happiness. And when sorrows surround us, we sin by equating happiness with holiness.

We are so quickly drawn into being mad at God instead of trusting him. When are we going to stop equating pain with God's punishment and turn our anger into surrender?

Please don't let Satan stop you on your path to repentance.

CHAPTER 5

Fear: I Am Afraid

❧❧

"For behold what earnestness this very thing, this godly sorrow, has produced in you: what vindication of yourselves, what indignation, what fear, what longing, what zeal, what avenging of wrong! In everything you demonstrated yourselves to be innocent in the matter" (II Corinthians 7:11).

God, who breathed the world into existence, can breathe us out of existence. God, who forges relationships with the power of his love, can dissolve them with the power of his judgment.

My wife, the keeper of the alarm clock, had set the music to come on per my request. I had an early meeting, and I needed to change my usual routine. Jana's schedule is to rise early, then go to another room to have her quiet time. When the alarm sounded, I awoke and looked at the time. It was an hour earlier than what I was expecting. So I reached across the bed to reset it. In my semiconscious state, I hit a button called "sleep." After that, there was no way to turn the radio off. I tried to change the alarm time. I tried to change the actual time. I tried turning it off. I even tried unplugging it which then erased all the time settings. I was getting frustrated, so I called out for the keeper of the clock.

"Jana, help me. Jana!"

"Yes?"

"Come help me."

She was there as quickly as she could get there. "What's the matter? Are you okay?"

"I can't get this stupid clock to reset. Can you help me?"

She grabbed me in her arms and began to kiss my cheek. "Is that all? I thought you were having a heart attack. Your cry sounded like you were in real trouble." She feared a possible loss. She was afraid that I would be taken from her.

After she fixed the alarm and went back to her quiet time, I lay in bed and began to think. Just as I was unable to fix the clock, I am often unable to fix my relationship with God. My sin separates me from my heavenly Father. When I fear a possible loss of relationship with my God because of my sin, do I run as quickly as I can to God and find out what I need to do to relieve my fear of separation?

Fear: I Am Afraid

The next word for us to consider on our journey to repentance is *fear*. The Greek word is the normal word that is used for fear. It is the word *phobos,* from which we derived our English word *phobia.*

God has led us to repentance. The Holy Spirit has revealed to us the destructiveness of sin. He has also placed within those who are seeking restoration a desire to negate the effects of sin upon their lives. He has allowed us to deal with the sorrow we feel when we have been seduced by Satan. Our intellect is interacting with our emotions, and it is producing vulnerability. That unsettling influence can quickly lead to fear. Fear on the pathway to repentance is not something that you reject. It is something that you experience and allow to move you back toward God. God is our strength. He is our fortress. He is our Savior and Lord.

In our focal passage, godly sorrow leads to fear. Just as love can influence us in a myriad of ways, fear can also. There are all kinds of ways that fear manifests itself: fear of a broken relationship, fear of God's punishment, fear of an addiction, fear of a missed blessing, fear of separation, fear of losing control, fear of intensified pain, or fear of succumbing to more temptation.

Each one has the possibility of moving us away from God or moving us toward him.

Fear of a broken relationship: One evening my nineteen-year-old daughter left on a trip from Austin, Texas to Dallas, Texas, about 180 miles away. Taking the trip in the evening hours made her mother and me very apprehensive. Haley had a cell phone, so I thought that if anything happened she could call and I would either go get her or help alleviate the problem. She had been gone for over two hours, so I decided to call and see where she was. When she answered the phone, she seemed agitated, and said she had to go and would call me back and hung up. Well, the meter in my mind went to worry very quickly. I called her back immediately. This time she seemed even more agitated, and I could hear some commotion in the back ground. It sounded like a male voice. She said, "Dad, I can't talk right now." She hung up again. Well, by this time, I'm thinking she has been abducted. (Sometimes I can make big jumps.) I called her back her back immediately, and she did not answer. God and I began to have a real heart-to-heart talk. I began crying out to God, asking him to protect her. I called her again, and there was no answer. Fear gripped my soul. I was about to call the highway patrol. I tried one more time, and this time she answered.

I immediately began my inquisition. "Are you okay? Is there anything wrong? I was about to call the police." With a quivering voice she said, "Don't worry, Dad, they are here. I just got a speeding ticket, and the police officer was getting mad at me because the phone was ringing, so I had to cut it off."

I can tell you that this situation produced one of the most honest conversations I have ever had with God. I was pleading for his grace upon my daughter. My fear was driving me to God.

When I sin, it produces the possibility of great loss in my relationship with God. Why won't I let fear drive me into the hands of God? Most of us have had experiences where we are terribly afraid, and we let the outcome dictate whether we would stay in the hands of God or whether we push ourselves away. Our fear gets us to God, but our perception of the outcome determines whether we praise God and continue on his path or whether we will curse God and reject his influence.

The outcome of a repentant heart is to find times of refreshing. The fear of being separated from God can be one of the most powerful of all motivations. Where would we be without him? What if we called out to him and he did not answer? What if his love was conditional? What if he kept changing his mind? What if he rejected us?

When that kind of fear arises from our sin, do not hinder its affect. Let it drive you to restoration. Let it motivate you like the main characters were motivated in Luke 15: the young woman's fear of not finding her lost coin, the shepherd's fear of not finding his lost sheep, and the prodigal son's fear of being abandoned in a strange place. Go out and search. Search for that which was lost. Wait eagerly for the wooing of the Holy Spirit, and follow the Spirit's lead. When you come back to the Almighty, humble yourself in his presence, rejoice in his mercy, and continue your journey to the times of refreshing.

Fear of God's discipline: In my generation, spanking was often used. My mother's favorite method was to pull out her trusty flyswatter and go to work. There were four of us siblings, three boys and one girl. We boys could get rowdy at times. We used the house for our own wrestling ring. Mom would start out by giving us a warning. She would elevate her threats if we didn't respond. And finally, here she would come, swinging from the hip and taking no prisoners. In our younger days, we feared the punishment. In our older days, we feared she would get hurt. We gather as a family every Thanksgiving and we still hear, "You better cut it out. I'm going to get the flyswatter." And if we don't respond, my eighty-year-old mom will charge in and swing away.

When we sin, we know that God will discipline us.

"For they disciplined us for a short time as seemed best to them, but He disciplines us for our good, that we may share His holiness" (Hebrews 12:10).

"For those whom the Lord loves He disciplines" (Hebrews 12:6).

And sometimes the discipline can be severe. Somewhere in the pulpits of today we have lost the message of the discipline of God. We have made God our personal trainer. He is our instructor, but not our corrector. He disciples us, but he does not discipline us. He is our counselor and not our judge.

Read these next verses and let the severity of the message pierce your heart.

"For if we go on sinning willfully after receiving the knowledge of the truth, there no longer remains a sacrifice for sins, but a certain terrifying expectation of judgment, and the fury of a fire which will consume the adversaries. Anyone who has set aside the Law of Moses dies without mercy on the testimony of two or three witnesses. How much severer punishment do you think he will deserve who has trampled under foot the Son of God, and has regarded as unclean the blood of the covenant by which he was sanctified, and has insulted the Spirit of grace? For we know Him who said, 'Vengeance is Mine, I will repay.' And again, 'The Lord will judge His people. It is a terrifying thing to fall into the hands of the living God" (Hebrews 10:26–31).

God, who breathed the world into existence, can breathe us out of existence.

God, who made us so perfectly that we can experience the wonder of his creation, can alter our bodies so that we will experience pain.

God, who controls all circumstances, can engineer circumstances that will cause us to stop and consider our lifestyle.

God, who forges relationships with the power of his love, can dissolve them with the power of his judgment.

God, who owns the cattle on a thousand hills, can give that wealth—and he can take it away.

God hates sin. God will punish sin. Our sin carries consequences. God loves us so much that he will do anything to motivate us to seek him. And if we do not turn back to him, then we will have to face the consequences.

Fear God! Fear his wrath! Fear his punishment! It is terrifying to fall into the hands of the living Lord. Please don't think that it won't happen to you. Please don't think that somehow you will escape. Please don't believe that you are the exception. Let the knowledge of God's punishment produce in you a godly fear—one that will drive you back to him.

Fear of addiction: When I first met him, he was trying to find peace. He had been to the pinnacle of earthly pleasure, but had fallen into the abyss of its consequences. The shallowness of the earthly joys couldn't fill the depth of the void that was in his life. He wanted to break away, because he feared that if he continued in what he was doing, it would wind itself so tightly around him that he would never be able to escape.

Larry was a pimp. He had an escort service in Colorado. He had all the money he wanted. He had all the alcohol and drugs he wanted. He was nearing the top of Mt. Lust. But there was always a hole in his soul. There was always a yearning—a yearning produced by the memories of attending revival meetings when he was a child. These feelings would be deadened when he became intoxicated with the world. They were never eliminated. And there was always with him the thought that he would go too far. He would either kill or be killed.

Then he rediscovered the Christ of his childhood. His life was changed. He walked away. He was wide open to the grace and mercy of our Lord, because he understood that those things could break his addiction and set him free.

God can and does use the fear of possible consequences to draw us back to him. Do you remember the story of the beggar, Lazarus, and the rich man? Jesus tells it better than I do:

"Now there was a certain rich man, and he habitually dressed in purple and fine linen, gaily living in splendor every day. And a certain poor man named Lazarus was laid at his gate, covered with sores, and longing to be fed with the crumbs which were falling from the rich man's table; besides, even the dogs were coming and licking his sores. Now it came about that the poor man died and he was carried away by the angels to Abraham's bosom; and the rich man also died and was buried. And in Hades he lifted up his eyes, being in torment, and saw Abraham far away, and Lazarus in his bosom. And he cried out and said, 'Father Abraham, have mercy on me, and send Lazarus, that he may dip the tip of his finger in water and cool off my tongue; for I am in agony in this flame.' But Abraham said, 'Child, remember that during your life you received your good things, and likewise Lazarus bad things; but now he is being comforted here, and you are in agony. And besides all this, between us and you there is a great chasm fixed, in order that those who wish to come over from here to you may not be able, and that none may cross over from there to us.' And he said, 'Then I beg you, Father, that you send him to my father's house—for I have five brothers—that he may warn them, lest they also come to this place of torment.' But Abraham said, 'They have Moses and the Prophets; let them hear them.' But he said, 'No, Father Abraham, but if someone goes to them from the dead, they will repent!' But he said to him, 'If they do not listen to Moses and the

Prophets, neither will they be persuaded if someone rises from the dead'" (Luke 16:19–31).

The rich man was driven by a great fear for his brothers. He wanted them to know that their addiction to wealth would lead to eternal torment. But it was too late! Please allow God to open your eyes. Pray that He would open your eyes so that you may see what is before you. And if you are entwined in the tentacles of the world, repent!

Fear of a missed blessing: I know a young man who flunked his World Literature class three times. He had made so many attempts at graduation, only to fail, that his parents finally cut off the funds. And for this young man, no funds meant no school. To tell you the truth, his inability to pass World Literature wasn't because he was incapable of passing. He was simply too lazy.

That same young man met a young lady, and they fell in love. He proposed to her. And she said, "No." He was working at a sporting goods store making minimum wage. "You cannot even support yourself with this job, how are you going to support us if we get married?"

It is amazing how the fear of missing out on something you want badly changes your motivation. He begged his parents for one more chance. He only lacked sixteen hours to graduate. After many heart-to-heart discussions, the parents decided to give him one more chance.

He went back to school and passed all sixteen hours. He took World Literature for a fourth time. He received an A. As a matter of fact, his grade point average for those last sixteen hours was a 4.0! He was so afraid that he would fail that he wanted to make sure there was no doubt. His fear of losing the love and respect of this young lady changed his life.

We have a wonderful blessing that awaits us. God has prepared a place where we are set free from the restraints of this world. Here are some other blessings that await us:

We will have the same glorious body as our Lord. "Who will transform the body of our humble state into conformity with the body of His glory, by the exertion of the power that He has even to subject all things to Himself" (Philippians 3:21).

Picture in your mind the description of our Lord recorded in John's Revelation. "And in the middle of the lamp stands one like a son of man, clothed in a robe reaching to the feet, and girded across His breast with a golden girdle. And His head and His hair were white like white wool, like snow; and His eyes were like a flame of fire; and His feet were like burnished bronze, when it has been caused to glow in a furnace, and His voice was like the sound of many waters. And in His right hand He held seven stars; and out of His mouth came a sharp two-edged sword; and His face was like the sun shining in its strength" (Revelation 1:13–16).

That certainly is a body of glory. Scripture says that those who are children of God will have a body like that. It will be glorious. There is no telling what it will be like. What an absolutely wonderful day that will be.

We will enjoy the riches of his grace and kindness forever. "But God, being rich in mercy, because of His great love with which He loved us, even when we were dead in our transgressions, made us alive together with Christ (by grace you have been saved), and raised us up with Him, and seated us with Him in the heavenly places, in Christ Jesus, in order that in the ages to come He might show the surpassing riches of His grace in kindness toward us in Christ Jesus" (Ephesians 2:4–7).

When you think about the grace God has demonstrated here on this earth, when you think about the grace he has demonstrated to those he loves, and when you think about the grace he has demonstrated in your life, you must be in awe. And then realize that God will demonstrate that grace to you for all eternity.

When you think about the examples of kindness that Jesus displayed while he was here on the earth, does that not move you toward him?

Who wouldn't feel blessed in the presence of a man who loved the children, who physically touched lepers to heal them, who stopped a funeral procession to give back an only son to a grieving widow, who knelt down to raise up a woman caught in adultery just so he could look her in the eyes and make sure she understood that she was forgiven, who made sure that a woman who had been sick for so long understood the healing brought about by her faith, and who even included others from outside the Jewish people?

His kindness leads to repentance!

We will have an eternal dwelling place that exceeds anything on earth. So many people are drawn to the stories of the "rich and famous." An opulent lifestyle appeals directly to our flesh. Living where there is no concern with having anything you want, living where you can receive the finest care possible, and living where the focus is entirely on yourself is something that most people are drawn to. But this lifestyle is only available to the smallest of minorities.

The Bible talks about a narrow road that leads to everlasting life and a broad road that leads to destruction. This would indicate that more will miss the road than find it. It will be a smaller minority—but much larger than the one that contains the rich and famous.

God has prepared a more magnificent home for the small group that finds the narrow road. John seeks to describe it in earthly terms: "And I saw a new heaven and a new earth; for the first heaven and the first earth passed away, and there is no longer any sea. And I saw the holy city, new Jerusalem, coming down out of heaven from God, made ready as a bride adorned for her husband. And I heard a loud voice from the throne, saying, 'Behold, the tabernacle of God is among men, and He shall dwell among them, and they shall be His people, and God Himself shall be among them, and He shall wipe away every tear from their eyes; and there shall no longer be any death; there shall no longer be any mourning, or crying, or pain; the first things have passed away.' And He who sits on the throne said, 'Behold, I am making all things new.' And He said, 'Write, for these words are faithful and true.' And He said to me, 'It is done. I am the Alpha and the Omega, the beginning and the end. I will give to the one who thirsts from the spring of the water of life without cost. He who overcomes shall inherit these things, and I will be his God and he will be My son'" (Revelation 21:1–7, 10–23).

In this section of scripture, God promises us a new dwelling place. He promises that his tabernacle will be there—not only his tabernacle, but he himself! He promises us his comfort. There will no longer be any pain or suffering. He promises that we will be able to drink from the spring of the water of life without cost.

What wonderful things he has prepared for us—for those of us who make him our God.

Again John tries to describe the heavenly with earthly words: "And he carried me away in the Spirit to a great and high mountain, and showed me the Holy city, Jerusalem, coming down out of heaven from God, having the glory of God. Her brilliance was like a very costly stone, as a stone of crystal-clear jasper. It had a great and high wall, with twelve gates, and at the gates twelve angels; and names were written on them, which are those of the twelve tribes of the sons of Israel. There were three gates on the east and three gates on the north and three gates on the south and three gates on the west. And the wall of the city had twelve foundation stones, and on them were the twelve names of the twelve apostles of the Lamb. And the one who spoke with me had a gold measuring rod to measure the city, and its gates and its wall. And the city is laid out as a square, and its length is as great as the width; and he measured the city with the rod, fifteen hundred miles; its length and width and height are equal. And he measured its wall, seventy-two yards, according to human measurements, which are also angelic measurements. And the material of the wall was jasper; and the city was pure gold, like clear glass. The foundation stones of the city wall were adorned with every kind of precious stone. The first foundation stone was jasper; the second, sapphire; the third, chalcedony; the fourth, emerald; the fifth, sardonyx; the sixth, sardius; the seventh, chrysolite; the eighth, beryl; the ninth, topaz; the tenth, chrysoprase; the eleventh, jacinth; the twelfth, amethyst. And the twelve gates were twelve pearls; each one of the gates was a single pearl. And the street of the city was pure gold, like transparent glass. And I saw no temple in it, for the Lord God, the Almighty, and the Lamb, are its temple. And the city has no need of the sun or of the moon to shine upon it, for the glory of God has illumined it, and its lamp is the Lamb" (Revelation 21:10–23).

What we consider precious here on this earth, God uses as building material. What we crave, he paves roads with. What we string together and hang around our neck as a symbol of wealth, he builds gates with. What we covet to put into rings, bracelets, and necklaces, he builds a foundation with. Gold and precious stones will be so common that they will lose their value. We will surrounded by the finest things that we have ever been exposed to.

And closing his writings in the book of Revelation, John attempts one more time to describe heaven: "And he showed me a river of the water of life, clear as crystal, coming from the throne of God and of the Lamb, in the middle of its street. And on either side of the river was the tree of life, bearing twelve kinds of fruit, yielding its fruit every month; and the leaves of the tree were for the healing of the nations. And there shall no longer be any curse; and the throne of God and of the Lamb shall be in it, and His bond-servants shall serve Him; and they shall see His face, and His name shall be on their foreheads. And there shall no longer be any night; and they shall not have need of the light of a lamp nor the light of the sun, because the Lord God shall illumine them; and they shall reign forever and ever" (Revelation 22:1–5).

There is one phrase in this passage that really captures my attention. John writes, "And there shall no longer be any curse." I am so thankful that God has promised to his believers that we will be able to live with him throughout all eternity free from the curse of sin!

Instead of death, there will be life.

Instead of darkness, there will be light.

Instead of pain, there will be comfort.

Instead of loneliness, there will be presence.

Instead of want, there will be plenty.

When you consider the alternative, who would choose not to go to heaven? Do not miss the blessing. Repentance is that narrow road that leads to an everlasting life in the presence of God.

Are you going there?

This is how you can know that you will a citizen of heaven one day:

A. Accept the fact that God loves you so much that he allowed his Son, Jesus Christ, to pay the penalty for your sin. "For while we were still helpless, at the right time Christ died for the ungodly" (Romans 5:6). "But God demonstrates His own love toward us, in that while we were yet sinners, Christ died for us" (Romans 5:8).

B. Put your faith and your trust in Jesus, who loves you so. "For by grace you have been saved through faith; and that not of yourselves, it is the gift of God" (Ephesians 2:8). "Therefore having been justified by faith, we have peace with God through our Lord Jesus Christ" (Romans 5:1).

C. Submit to the Lordship of Jesus Christ. "But thanks be to God, who gives us the victory through our Lord Jesus Christ" (1 Corinthians 15:57). "Thomas answered and said to Him, 'My Lord and my God!'" (John 20:28)

D. Pray and ask Jesus Christ to become your Savior and Lord.

You might want to pray a prayer like this: "Dear Lord Jesus, thank you so much for loving me. Thank you for allowing me mercy. I know I have sinned. And it is the desire of my heart to turn away from sin. I believe you were God's son, and that you lived on this earth to show me how to act. I believe that you died on the cross as a payment for my sins. I ask you to take control of my life. I submit to you as my Savior and Lord. Live through me. Amen.

We are not able to conceive all that God has for us. "But just as it is written, 'Things which eye has not seen and ear has not heard, and which have not entered the heart of man, all that God has prepared for those who love Him'" (1 Corinthians 2:9).

"Now to Him who is able to do exceeding abundantly beyond all that we ask or think, according to the power that works within us" (Ephesians 3:20).

Here in these two verses, Paul writes that we do not have the ability to conceive what heaven will be like. Do you remember the words of Paul in II Corinthians 12? "I know a man in Christ who fourteen years ago—whether in the body I do not know, or out of the body I do not know, God knows—such a man was caught up to the third heaven. And I know how such a man—whether in the body or apart from the body I do not know, God knows—was caught up into Paradise, and heard inexpressible words, which a man is not permitted to speak. On behalf of such a man will I boast; but on my own behalf I will not boast, except in regard to my weaknesses. For if I do wish to boast I shall not be foolish, for I shall be speaking the truth; but I refrain from this, so that no one may credit me with more than he sees in me or hears from me. And because of the surpassing greatness of the revelations, for this reason, to keep me from exalting myself, there was given me a thorn in the flesh, a messenger of Satan to buffet me—to keep me from exalting myself!"

It is easy to deduce from this passage of scripture that Paul was the one who was called up into heaven. He says that we are not even able to conceptualize the glory of heaven. When you think about it, that is easy to accept.

My family and I had the wonderful privilege of taking summer vacations. We didn't have much money but we had a minivan and a pop-up camper. And every summer, while the children were young, we would put some miles on that van. In the spring, the planning began. We would map out a route. I can remember not being very excited about going to the Grand Canyon or Mt. Rushmore. After all, I had seen hundreds of pictures of both of them. What more was there?

Words cannot explain my first experience of looking over the south rim of the Grand Canyon or looking into the faces on Mt. Rushmore. Pictures just did not do it justice. I was in awe. My senses were overwhelmed. The magnificence was too large for me to wrap my mind around. "How?" was a prominent question. Those of you who have shared similar experiences know what I am talking about. Those who have not are like humans when we speak of heaven. We have heard all the earthly descriptive words—but until we see it, we cannot reproduce the awe.

This is available. Don't miss the blessing. Let your desire lead you to repentance.

FEAR OF SEPARATION

It was 11:30 pm when the call came. She lasted longer than we expected. It was her first time to spend the night with a friend. When I went to pick her up, I got the report from her friend's parents. "We tried to comfort her, but she kept saying, 'I want my mommy.' After hearing that many, many times, we decided to call."

We walked to the car in silence. "Are you okay?"

"Yes."

"Why didn't you stay?"

"I was afraid."

"That's all right." We drove on in silence. When I pulled the car into the garage, I looked over, and she was sound asleep.

She changed from a state of high anxiety to the peaceful state of slumber. She was back in the presence of the ones who take care of her, who protect her, and who love her.

For those who have developed a deep relationship with God through Jesus, it is devastating when they sense a break in relationship. The words of our Lord when he says "I will never leave you nor will I forsake you" are words that restore relationship. They are the words of the one who can calm the soul—no matter what the age.

All of us sin, no matter how long we have walked with God and no matter how much we desire to please him. And repentance is necessary.

My wife and I have been married over thirty years. I fear separation, the times when she goes her way and I go mine. I fear the awkwardness that fills the house as we work through the problem. I fear the uneasiness when she and I search for words and actions that will restore. It is a fear of separation. That fear leads us to reconciliation. We have been together far too long and love each other far too deeply to let the separation continue.

My Lord and I have been in the same family for almost fifty years. He has proven to be a wonderful companion, a great teacher, a strong protector, a merciful judge, a fair disciplinarian, a needed encourager, a faithful guide, and a compassionate friend. But because of my sinful nature, there are breaks in our relationship. And when those breaks come, it sends a chill through my soul. I want desperately to be restored. I want the rift to be healed. And my Savior leads me to the instructions of the Holy Spirit. And if I listen very closely, I will hear the call to repent.

My dear brothers and sisters, please listen for the call. Please follow the leadership of God's Spirit as it takes you down the path to peace. You will not find the "peace that passes all understanding" until you stop at the temple of repentance.

Fear of losing control

As he woke, the pain was almost unbearable. The throbbing felt as if someone was driving a nail through his skull. The pain was pushed back as he began to gain his bearings. He looked over at the spot where his wife usually laid, but the covers had been undisturbed. His listened for the voices of his children, but the house was unusually quiet. They were nowhere to be found. He remembered now. He remembered cussing at his wife as she grabbed the children's clothes, gathered the babies into her arms, and ran toward the car. He remembers running down the driveway, beating on the car, and threatening to find her and make her pay. The sad thing is that the images were not new. It seemed as if he was watching a terrible movie that he had seen several times before. As he moved through the house, he saw the broken dishes. He saw the hole in the sheetrock where he had thrown a glass pitcher. As his mind began to fully function, he was faced with the dreadful images of the night before.

His children crying and begging him to stop.

The look of terror as he lunged toward their mother.

The fear that gripped his wife when he grabbed her and pushed her to the floor.

The look of rage on his face when he caught himself in the mirror.

How could he act like that? How could he completely lose control? Was there any way that he could restore his family? Would he ever be able to show her that he did truly love her? Is this the time that she would leave and never look back?

The fear of losing control can finally drive a person to repentance. Maybe it is the fear of lost control. God provides a way for us to overcome!

"For whatever is born of God overcomes the world; and this is the victory that has overcome the world—our faith" (1 John 5:4)

Our faith in the ways of God will give us the strength to be victorious. Our trust in the power of the Almighty to transform our lives will prove our success!

We can have faith in our Lord to overcome, because he has overcome.

"These things I have spoken to you, that in Me you may have peace. In the world you have tribulation, but take courage; I have overcome the world" (John 16:33).

Jesus fought the battles and won. His skirmish with fear lasted only as long as he felt separated from his Father.

His fight with his anger as he looked into the temple-turned-market was controlled by his love for holiness, not revenge.

His contempt for the disciples when they didn't seem able to grasp the heart of his message was subdued by his vision of what they would become.

His clash with indulgence as Satan laid before him the riches of humanity was alleviated when he feasted on the word of his Father, not the wisdom of the world.

His combat with the nerves in his body screaming with pain as he hung on the cross, drawing him closer to giving up, were conquered by his love for you and me.

Jesus overcame. And he has given us the power to do likewise. Remember these words: "You are from God, little children, and have overcome them; because greater is He who is in you than he who is in the world" (1 John 4:4).

Fear can be a great motivating factor. Let us fear any break in our relationship with the Lord, the source of our refreshing.

Chapter 6

Longing: I Long for God

✦ ✦

"For behold what earnestness this very thing, this godly sorrow, has produced in you: what vindication of yourselves, what indignation, what fear, what longing, what zeal, what avenging of wrong! In everything you demonstrated yourselves to be innocent in the matter" (II Corinthians 7:11).

This point along the continuum of repentance is crucial! So many people get to this point and fall back because they follow the wisdom of man rather than the word of God.

Have you ever heard of Pee Wee Football? Pee Wee Football was the title for the organized league for fourth-, fifth-, and sixth-graders in our small Texas town. It is the league where one kid can weigh fifty pounds and another kid can weigh 120. It is the league where the team with the fastest kid wins 75% of all the games. It is the league where the biggest boy plays running back so the 120-pound boy can carry all the fifty-pound boys down the field until one of the small boys gets tangled up in the ball carrier's legs.

I know a little boy who played in that league. He was in the fourth grade. It had been a long season. His team hadn't won a game. He played defensive back. I'm not sure if he even weighed fifty pounds. Near the end of the season, this little boy, who was out on the field playing defensive back and hoping that the 120-pound boy or the fast boy didn't come his way, began to cry. I mean, he was crying out loud. His teammates thought he was hurt and called a time-out. The coach sent another boy in, and the little one ran to the sideline.

He was met by the coach. "What's the matter?"

"Nothing."

"Are you hurt?"

"No."

"Then what is the matter?"

The little boy hung his head and started crying again. "I just want to win."

I know that little boy fairly well. That little boy was me. Oh, how I longed to win. I was tired of getting beaten time after time. I was tired of getting tangled up in the big boy's legs. I was tired of chasing the fastest boy and never catching him. Maybe I could have handled it a lot better if we had won every once in a while.

LONGING: I LONG FOR GOD

There is strong emotion in the meaning of this word, longing.

Have you ever been very, very lonely and longed for companionship? That is the strength of this word.

Have you ever been ill for a long time and longed for relief, just a moment of relief? That is the strength of this word.

Have you ever been separated from the one you love and longed to be in their presence one more time? That is the strength of this word.

There is a wonderful example of this in the Bible. It is found in Luke 15.

The word *longing* carries with it an implication of lacking something. The Holy Spirit knows that we lack peace, that we lack restoration, and that we lack motivation. The Holy Spirit knows our needs and wants to use our natural emotions to draw us back to God. So the Spirit brings to mind those components of godly sorrow and how they reveal our deficiency.

This becomes evident when we look at the life of the prodigal son. In Luke 15, we find this wonderful story Jesus told:

"And He said to them, a man had two sons. The younger one said to his father, 'Father, give me my share of the estate.' So he divided his property between them.

Not long after that, the younger son got together all he had, set off for a distant country and there squandered his wealth in wild living. After he had spent everything, there was a severe famine in that whole country, and he began to be in need. So he went and hired himself out to a citizen of that country, who sent him to his fields to feed pigs. He longed to fill his stomach with the pods that the pigs were eating, but no one gave him anything.

When he came to his senses, he said, 'How many of my father's hired men have food to spare, and here I am starving to death! I will set out and go back to my father and say to him: Father, I have sinned against heaven and against you. I am no longer worthy to be called your son; make me like one of your hired men.' So he got up and went to his father. But while he was still a long way off, his father saw him and was filled with compassion for him; he ran to his son, threw his arms around him and kissed him. The son said to him, 'Father, I have sinned against heaven and against you. I am no longer worthy to be called your son.' But the father said to his servants, 'Quick! Bring the best robe and put it on him. Put a ring on his finger and sandals on his feet. Bring the fattened calf and kill it. Let's have a feast and celebrate. For this son of mine was dead and is alive again; he was lost and is found.' So they began to celebrate. Meanwhile, the older son was in the field. When he came near the house, he heard music and dancing. So he called one of the servants and asked him what was going on. 'Your brother has come,' he replied, 'and your father has killed the fattened calf because he has him back safe and sound.' The older brother became angry and refused to go in. So his father went out and pleaded with him. But he answered his father, 'Look! All these years I've been slaving for you and never disobeyed your orders. Yet you never gave me even a young goat so I could celebrate with my friends. But when this son of yours who has squandered your property with prostitutes comes home, you kill the fattened calf for him!' 'My son,' the father said, 'you are always with me, and everything I have is yours. But we had to celebrate and be glad, because this brother of yours was dead and is alive again; he was lost and is found'" (Luke 15:11–32).

As you look back on the story, it is not difficult to see the concern of the young man begin to surface. His bank account was dwindling. He was going to find another source of income, but he just never got around to it. The loose lifestyle really appealed to him, but how was he going to sustain it?

And then there were the conflicting thoughts. This is not what his father had taught him. This is not how his father had instructed him in dealing with his money. He could hear his dear father in the quietness of his soul.

"Son, there is nothing easy in this world."

"Son, remember it takes a long time to build wealth, but only a short time to lose it.

"Son, watch out for your friends. Make sure that they will still be there in the rough times."

"Son, if you trust God with everything you have, he will help you carefully guard it against those who want your money and don't care anything about you."

The concern continued to grow. He really did want to do something about it. At least that is what he told himself.

Then it happened. He went to his stash of money and it was all gone. Surely his new friends would understand that now it was their turn to pick up the tab. Surely they would stand by him, loan him some money. Surely they would stick with him until his fortune turned. But he learned the hard way that that was not the case. His new friends left as fast as they arrived. It was almost as if they were hounds of hell running off after the smell of new money.

Their departure reinforced the thoughts he had lately. He would make things right. He would vindicate himself in the eyes of his new countrymen. But the more he thought about that, the more he realized that it wasn't the countrymen that he wanted to make things right with. It was his father. How would he be able to do that? He wanted so desperately to have things back like they were before, but he didn't think that would ever happen. But surely there was something that could be done. He had to at least consider returning as one of the options. His attitude was turning from one of independence to one of humility.

But his pride kept him from starting home. He would find a job. And that he did. How many days do you think he lasted feeding the pigs? And how many times do you think he had this conversation: "I can't believe how stupid I've been! Why didn't I listen to my father? Why did I think that I could handle it, that I would be the one who made it? I just can't believe that I am in the midst of a foreign land, among a bunch of pigs, so hungry that I have to eat what they are eating."

His anger was growing. And when he wasn't angry, he was throwing the biggest pity party he could. He just couldn't believe his stupidity.

And it wasn't long before fear began to capture his soul. "I am going to starve to death. What if I am unable to get out of here? What if I die here and no one ever knows what happened to me? What if I never get to see my family again?"

Have you followed the progression?

The concern began to grow as the money disappeared. He knew that he would have to make some changes, and he became eager to make them.

He could never escape the influence of his father. He could never forget the words of wisdom that his father had told him over and over. The call to righteousness would not leave him alone.

And then there was the anger—the anger over his own stupidity, the anger over getting duped by so many people, the anger over not managing his money, the anger over failure.

Finally there was the fear. What if he had to stay in that pig pen forever? What if he died there?

All these factors led to a deep desire to change. He would go back to his father and ask to be a hired servant. They were treated better than he was being treated. "My father will treat me justly. My father will look past by failure. He has seen me work. I know I can do what the servants do. I will go to my father."

The longing spurred action—the action leading to restoration.

There was another incident in the life of Jesus that reflects a different outcome. The longing was there, but the response led him away from God instead of toward him.

"And behold, one came to Him and said, 'Teacher, what good thing shall I do that I may obtain eternal life?' And He said to him, 'Why are you asking Me about what is good? There is only One who is good; but if you wish to enter into life, keep the commandments.' He said to Him, 'Which ones?' And Jesus said, 'You shall not commit murder; You shall not commit adultery; You shall not steal; You shall not bear false witness; Honor your father and mother; and You shall love your neighbor as yourself.' The young man said to Him, 'All these things I have kept; what am I still lacking?'

Jesus said to him, 'If you wish to be complete, go and sell your possessions and give to the poor, and you shall have treasure in heaven; and come, follow Me.' But when the young man heard this statement, he went away grieved; for he was one who owned much property" (Matthew 19:16–22).

This young man certainly approached Jesus with earnestness. But his goal was not to be refreshed in the Lord. His goal was to be lauded for personal goodness. He wanted recognition rather than restoration.

And then there was the vindication. The wealthy young man had an eagerness to justify himself. He wanted Jesus to know how good he had been. He wanted all those around him to know that he kept the commandments—that he kept them from an early age.

And he was indignant, all right. He was indignant at all those who couldn't live up to his standards. He had achieved great things. Why couldn't the poor do the same thing?

When Jesus offered the rich man the opportunity of a lifetime, to travel with him and see the heavens open up, the man was filled with fear. It is true that those who have wealth have a great fear of losing it. His fear was not that he would not please Jesus. His fear was that he would not impress others.

After Jesus told him how he could free his heart, the young man was filled with longing—longing to get away from Jesus. Was the grieving an act? Did he have to put on a good show? Did he want others to think that it was a hard decision? There are so many emotions on the road to real repentance. But if those emotions don't lead to acts of faith, they do no more than mask the desperation.

Some long for God, and this leads to restoration. There are others that long for the wisdom of others, and this leads to destruction.

This point along the continuum of repentance is crucial! So many people get to this point and fall back because they follow the wisdom of other people rather than the word of God.

Read again the truths of God's word concerning man's wisdom: "There is a way which seems right to a man, but its end is the way of death" (Proverbs 14:12).

"For as the heavens are higher than the earth, so are My ways higher than your ways, and My thoughts than your thoughts" (Isaiah 55:9).

"Which things we also speak, not in words taught by human wisdom, but in those taught by the Spirit, combining spiritual thoughts with spiritual words" (I Corinthians 2:13).

"For the wisdom of this world is foolishness before God. For it is written, 'He is the one who catches the wise in their craftiness" (I Corinthians 3:19).

"Where is the wise man? Where is the scribe? Where is the debater of this age? Has not God made foolish the wisdom of the world?" (I Corinthians 1:20).

"For our proud confidence is this, the testimony of our conscience, that in holiness and godly sincerity, not in fleshly wisdom but in the grace of God, we have conducted ourselves in the world, and especially toward you" (II Corinthians 1:12).

One day Paul came to see me. Paul was separated from his wife and living with another woman. It was the same woman that he had had an affair with two years earlier. He came to talk with me about his wife's actions. She would not let her son even be around him. She certainly wouldn't allow their sixteen-year-old son to come over to the house where he was living with his lover. Paul put it me this way, "She's using God in the wrong way. She is keeping my son away from me."

And then he began to justify his lifestyle. "I go to church quite often. I pray. I even tithe. I watch a megachurch preacher on the television." Paul just couldn't figure out why his wife was acting like she was.

It didn't occur to him that his blatant disregard for the Bible's stance on adultery could be interfering with his desires. He did a lot of good things. Didn't that offset the sinful relationship that he was living in? And shouldn't others see his goodness and forget about the rest? "I am happy," he said. "Doesn't God want me to be happy?"

Because I had a good relationship with Paul, I was able to talk with him about God's holiness. We were friends. He listened. The more we talked, the more his sin was brought to light, and the more he felt the weight of his transgression. I talked to him about repentance and his need to truly restore his relationship with God. I told him that I would walk with him, disciple him, and help him to gain the victory.

You could tell that there was a longing for a redeemed life. As the tears fell from his cheeks, the fake happiness disappeared. "Will you do it God's way?" I asked.

He got up and walked toward the door. He just shook his head and left.

Paul had bought into man's wisdom. He was happy. At least he had convinced himself that the world's pleasures were the same as happiness. He was so close to moving toward God, he was longing for real restoration. But Satan won that round. I do hope and pray that there is another.

Emotions are wonderful motivators. But they must be followed with action.

CHAPTER 7

Zeal: I Will Do it God's Way

❧❧

"For behold what earnestness this very thing, this godly sorrow, has produced in you: what vindication of yourselves, what indignation, what fear, what longing, what zeal, what avenging of wrong! In everything you demonstrated yourselves to be innocent in the matter" (II Corinthians 7:11).

She finally got to the end of herself, and that is where she found Jesus.

I see them around town all the time. They come in all different sizes and shapes. And every time I see another one, I secretly wish that I could do that. I know it would help me. I know how much I need it. Whenever I even make a small attempt to do it, it ends in defeat. I have on many occasions longed to be able to do what I see them doing. I have even made plans in my mind to join them. I've thought about how I would achieve this secret goal of mine. I truly have a deep desire to be able to run for distance.

But at this point, that is all I have, a deep desire. My heart is there. I would really like to be able to run. I have dreamed of running a 5K, a 10K, or even a marathon. Our family read a book by Ann Kiemel in which she described how she began to train and in less than two years was able to run a marathon. I think that people who are able to run that far are in great shape. And the athletic part of me wants to be in that kind of shape.

Some of you are asking yourself this question, "If he wants to do it so badly, then why doesn't he discipline himself and do it?"

There are so many of us who commit sin that we do not want to do. In fact, we long for control and purity. But as much as we long for it, we never do much more than that. And maybe God is asking that same question—"If you want to live a life that conquers sin, then why don't you do something about it?"

The goal of our study is to lead us to time of refreshing. Remember Acts 3:19? "Repent therefore and return, that your sins may be wiped away, in order that times of refreshing may come from the presence of the Lord" (Acts 3:19).

ZEAL: I WILL DO IT GOD'S WAY

The next step in our progression toward repentance is zeal.

The first two steps in repentance are earnestness and vindication. When we understand these two principles, we establish God's direction for renewal. They give us the right course, the right teaching. Those two prepare our mind and start us on our way. We learn the effects of sin, and we run to God eager to do something about them. We then learn God's way of making things right—how to vindicate ourselves. God teaches, and we listen.

Then the next three steps deal with our emotions. We wrestle with the problems caused by our sin, and we become disgusted. We are mad at what we have done. The severity of the situation produces fear in us—fear caused by the knowledge that we are fighting against an enemy that is far more powerful than we are, and so we long for God. We deeply desire to be under his watch and care.

Now we come to the last two steps to repentance—zeal and avenging of wrong. These two are an act of the will. No more teaching. No more motivation. It is time for action!

The Greek word for *zeal* is also translated as *jealousy*. It is a word that goes beyond the emotional element. It is a word that desires something as its own, and it is willing to take steps to get it. Zeal is the commitment to action and the preparation for doing so. The last fruit, avenging of wrong, is carrying out the decision made to act.

All of us know that there is a great difference between wanting to do something and actually doing it. The application of the word of God puts us in a position to see God's hand at work. Because we are human, our nature seems to draw us away from the doing of God's word. We need to act! What motivates us to act?

We are tired of the mess sin causes. "Therefore, since we have so great a cloud of witnesses surrounding us, let us also lay aside every encumbrance, and the sin which so easily entangles us, and let us run with endurance the race that is set before us" (Hebrews 12:1).

When we sin, there are consequences. And those consequences have claws. The devil makes sure that those claws dig deep into our soul. And he really doesn't care whether it is one fatal blow or a series of attacks. He wants you out of the game.

I watch a lot of animal shows on television. I especially like to watch the shows on Africa. I am intrigued by the battles that go on between the predators and their prey, like the wild dogs that hunt in a pack. They are not very big or very fast, but their endurance is unbelievable. They will pick out an animal and literally run the animal until the animal collapses. And all the time, they are nipping at the flanks. It is a tactic of wearing the animal down into submission. The leopard, on the other hand, strikes quickly. He often pounces on his prey from a tree. The prey, unaware that the leopard is in the tree, will walk right under the tree, and in less than a minute, the animal is dead. These predators are different, but they accomplish the same thing. Satan uses every tactic to bring us into submission. He will constantly hound us, or he will try to strike a fatal blow. He wants us destroyed and out of the war as an active soldier who is advancing God's kingdom.

There are times when a person gets tired of being the prey. Penny was tired of her life. She was in jail again. She tells this story:

"This last time in jail, I was trying something different. I had a lady from a local church mentoring me with some booklets that were developed by the church staff. She would come every Friday and answer my questions concerning the

Bible material that I didn't understand and give me more to work on. Well, jail was boring, so I tried.

"I knew about God and had some exposure to Jesus when I was little, but I had no idea what or how you could have a relationship with the unseen. One day, as I sat on my bunk and watched out the window as this crippled lady drug her crutches in 102-degree heat to come see me, I started crying, saying to myself, 'I am not worth it. I am not worth her time. Why would she do this for me?' Then I had a real understanding of why Christ got up on that cross. Even when I was whoring and shooting drugs, he still loved me and wanted me. He could see something in me that I didn't even know was there. I was tired of my life. God helped me.

"I have been clean and sober for eight years. I have been married to the same man for ten years. Chaos is kept at arm's length by my redeemer. He has given me purpose. I head a non-profit resource center for those coming from incarceration or drug treatment programs. I help them get plugged in to nurturing churches or recovery groups. He has given me a place. I have been an active member of my church for seven years and have helped in starting four different ministries. He has given me meaning. I am satisfied. I counsel and mentor others. I get the privilege to share in those small victories, and I lay my head down at night praising God for taking an old reprobate like me to use for *his* glory and purpose."

When Penny saw the love of this precious lady who would come and see her even though it was a great struggle, she was broken. The love of God transformed her from being hunted by Satan to being God's hunter, seeking out those to whom she could show God's love. She finally got to the end of herself. That is where she found Jesus. He motivated her to change.

Are you tired of the mess you are in? God can deliver! In Jesus's early ministry, he became so well-known for his healing that people would crowd around him. There were so many people that at times, Jesus and his disciples didn't even have time to eat. In chapter three of Mark's gospel, Jesus asked his disciples to have a boat prepared so that he could separate himself from the crowd: "For He had healed many, with the result that all those who had afflictions pressed about Him in order to touch Him" (Mark 3:10).

The primary meaning of the word that is translated *afflictions* is the word meaning *to whip*. Mark was saying that all those who felt they had been whipped by life could come to Jesus for healing. There is no problem too difficult for Jesus Christ. Please do not stop here. God wants to touch your life. Continue to receive the times of refreshing. You can overcome!

Another way we are motivated to change is through experiencing a deeper love for God. "I have been crucified with Christ; and it is no longer I who live, but Christ lives in me; and the life which I now live in the flesh I live by faith in the Son of God, who loved me, and delivered Himself up for me" (Galatians 2:20).

The old man sat alone. Day after day he would roll himself out on the porch and sit until the weather would force him back in. The deep wrinkles around his eyes and the pronounced furrows on his brow gave the indication that his life had been rough. And it had been. His drinking had cost him his family. His wife and children had left because of his abuse and abandonment. He was alone. He was filled with guilt. He was dying inside as well as outside. The only contact he had with people was the interaction with the staff of the nursing home. They tried to engage him, but were always rebuked by his silence. No one could penetrate his personal hell.

And then one day, his daughter showed up. His daughter had recently come to know Jesus as her Savior. She was hungry for the truth. She soaked in the scripture as if it was absolutely necessary for her existence. She listened to songs of praise. She was at the church every time the doors were open so she could learn more. Christ had reached down and given her forgiveness and hope. She just couldn't get enough. Then one day, she came across these verses:

"For if you forgive men for their transgressions, your heavenly Father will also forgive you. But if you do not forgive men, then your Father will not forgive your transgressions" (Matthew 6:14–15).

"And be kind to one another, tender-hearted, forgiving each other, just as God in Christ also has forgiven you" (Ephesians 4:32).

After reading these verses, the Holy Spirit and the devil began a battle in her soul. She immediately thought of her dad. And Satan made sure that all the sins that he had committed against her and her mom surfaced once again. But he didn't stop there. He brought up all the hatred she had held in her heart. She not only remembered the times of extreme pain but the plans she made for revenge. Surely God didn't expect her to go to her dad and try to reconcile. But the scripture would not go away. Forgive, and God will forgive. She certainly needed forgiveness herself. Be kind; forgive just as God has forgiven you. She knew she had to find her dad.

As the old man sat on the porch that day, a car drove up that he hadn't seen before. His eyes naturally followed it until it came to a stop. As the person got out, a wave of pure emotion rushed through his body. Was it his daughter? It sure looked like her—but it had been so long.

His daughter immediately recognized her father sitting on the porch. She approached very slowly and humbly.

"Dad—is that you, Dad?"

"Yes, my child, it's me."

"Dad, may I join you?"

"Oh, please do."

"Dad, I have become a Christian. I know that Jesus loves me and has forgiven me of my sin."

Her father just hung his head. Forgiveness—oh, how he had searched for forgiveness. He had cried out in his spirit a thousand times, asking for forgiveness. But of course, there was no reply.

"Dad, will you look at me?"

He slowly raised his head. Was she going to preach at him? Was she going to tell him all the sins that he had committed? Was she going to tell him that he needed God?

"Dad, God has forgiven me, and I am so thankful. I want you to know that I have forgiven you, and I ask you to forgive me for all the times I treated you disrespectfully. Will you forgive me?

Tears began to flow in both the father's and the daughter's eyes. The words that he had yearned to hear all these years echoed in his soul. "I forgive you." Those words were the keys that opened the door to his heart. He couldn't speak. He just cried. It was a long time before his first words were understandable through the sobs. "I'm so sorry. I'm so sorry. There was no need for you to ask me to forgive you, but I will."

The daughter had discovered God's love. She had gained God's forgiveness. She was open to the leadership of the Holy Spirit. And because she wanted to express her love for God by being obedient, even in the most difficult of situations, God was glorified.

Do you love God? I am not talking about submitting to God because you are afraid of judgment. I am not talking about being filled with thanksgiving for what God did for you through the sacrifice of his Son. I am not talking about the comfort that can be yours through the ministry of the Holy Spirit. I am talking about loving him so much that you are willing to lay aside your feelings and pursue those things that please him. I am talking about the continual realization of the depth of God's love and wanting to return that same kind of love. I am talking about loving him in such a way that puts him first.

There are many dimensions to God's love. We love God because he completes us. This is very similar to the love we have for our spouse. It is the love that wants the object of that love to be joined to them in pure *koinonia,* or fellowship of the soul. Our love grows in this manner when we spend time giving and receiving those things that build relationships.

We love God because he has nurtured us. This is very similar to the love that develops between parents and children. My mother and father are in their eighties. As I look back over my life and see the sacrifices they made for me, I truly want to do what I can to meet their needs. I want to nurture them as they did me. God has nurtured us. He was there to give us life. He was there to teach us the basis of our relationships. He was there to pick us up when we fell. He was there to comfort us and encourage us. He was there to do all he could to bring us to maturity. Our love grows when we respond to his nurture. Our love grows when we seek to serve him rather than be served.

Do you love God so deeply that you want to return his love?

We are motivated to change because we respect His stature. "He restores my soul; He guides me in the paths of righteousness For His name's sake" (Psalms 23:3 NAS).

There are people we know who stand for righteousness. They will not be swayed by others. They have accepted Jesus as their Lord and Savior, and they are like beacons in a dark world. When we wander off course, we can look to these people and make a course correction. They are gladiators in the arena of life. They bear the sword of the word of God and stand in the gap between holiness and licentiousness. The more we observe them, the more admiration, respect, and love we have for them. God is like that. He is the rock. He is the standard of which there is no variation. He stands firm, and there will be no shifting when the world puts him under scrutiny. Love grows, because we can always count on Him being the same. Love grows, because he is always holy, always righteous, always blameless, always honest, and always honorable.

When you have climbed out of the miry clay and found refuge on the solid rock, you appreciate the strong foundation.

The more we experience the love of God, the more we will obey, even in the hard work of repentance.

We are motivated to change when we see God at work and when we are privileged enough to be a minor partner in what God is doing. "Truly, truly, I say to you, he who believes in Me, the works that I do shall he do also; and greater works than these shall he do; because I go to the Father" (John 14:12 NAS).

One Sunday evening I was walking around the congregation greeting people as I usually do. I approached John. He asked me if I had heard the latest news on Alan. Alan was a young man who had already had two brain surgeries. "They have found two more spots on Alan's brain. It doesn't look good." I thanked John for telling me, and I began to look for Alan. The service started without us making contact.

After the service, as my wife Jana and I were leaving, my son approached and needed Jana to go with him to retrieve a car. They left quickly, so I lingered, still looking for Alan. Finally I spotted him. There were people around him, but the time came when we were able to talk. We spoke briefly, and I prayed for him. "I wanted to see you today," Alan said. "I looked for you this morning, but I just figured you haven't made it back from the holiday. You are not here right now by accident. I asked God to let me see you."

On the way home, I thought about what had happened. I was a part of an answered prayer. There was a great joy in my heart. Alan was in need. He wanted me to pray for him. It was easy to see God's hand in what happened. God let me approach John, and John gave me the information about Alan that I was not aware of. Jana left quickly with my son so I could linger. I would have left without seeing Alan if I had not stayed behind. Then I was able to go to Alan and pray for him. And after the prayer, he told me that he had prayed that he would see me. I was able to give encouragement. But I received much more than I gave. I just love to be a part of what God is doing!

People seeking restoration are so rare. Everyone is so quick to blame others. Many rationalize away the conviction of the Holy Spirit. But if we are obedient to do what God requires us to do, we have the chance to be an agent of change! We have a chance to join God in his redemptive work. We have a chance to be a doer of God's word and not just a hearer.

There are still some people who, when confronted with the truths of God, seek to change and conform to God's ways because their character still matters to them. "Though He slay me, I will hope in Him" (Job 13:15).

I am so thankful that there are still many who chose what is true, not what is appealing. Their motivation to change comes from a desire to be known as one who is willing to suffer for what is right.

In preparing to come to my parents' sixtieth wedding anniversary, I notified our children who were in college of our plan to come pick them up and then go to the party. When I shared that with my son, his response startled me. "Dad, I don't think I am going to go to the celebration." I knew what was behind his proposed change of plans. He had been invited to the home opener of the University of Texas football team. There were going to be over 80,000 fans. His high school classmate and friend was the starting fullback. He would be with his college buddies. The place would be rocking! He loves Texas football. He was displaying his emotional love. Before anything else was said, I replied, "T, this is your grandparents' sixtieth wedding anniversary. All of our family will be there. Your grandparents will be extremely disappointed." "Oh, okay, I am going with you." He demonstrated volitional love. What was right prevailed over what was more stimulating. He chose what he needed to do. It mattered to him that his grandparents saw him there. He cared about his character.

Men, this should resonate in your hearts. My wife and I have read the book *Love and Respect,* by Dr. Emerson Eggerichs. In the book, Dr. Eggerichs makes the point that men need unconditional respect in the same manner that women need unconditional love. As I read his presentation of the truths that had been revealed to him, my heart was saying, "Yes! Yes! Yes!" Oh, how I want my wife to respect me. I want my children to respect me. I want my friends to respect me. I want those I work with to respect me. Acting in a manner where one stands firmly in the will of God breeds respect. And most of all, I want God to respect me.

Do you remember the conversation that God had with Satan over Job? "And the Lord said to Satan, 'Have you considered My servant Job? For there is no one like him on the earth, a blameless and upright man, fearing God and turning away from evil'" (Job 1:8). Oh, that God might think that way about me. It was obvious that God respected Job. Don't you want to live your life in such a way that God would say something like that about you?

We must act! Are you tired of the mess sin causes in your life? Have you experienced the depth of God's love, and do you want to return that love through your obedience? Have you found in God that rock that will not be moved, one that stands for what is holy and pure? Have you been used by God, and do you desire to be more directly involved in his kingdom's work, knowing that a transformed life is a powerful tool in his hands? Does your character matter to you? Follow through!

CHAPTER 8

Avenging of Wrong: I Will Clear My Name

❧-❧

"For behold what earnestness this very thing, this godly sorrow, has produced in you: what vindication of yourselves, what indignation, what fear, what longing, what zeal, what avenging of wrong! In everything you demonstrated yourselves to be innocent in the matter" (II Corinthians 7:11).

"I'm old-school. I talked to him, and if he wants to talk to me, he can call." When it comes to avenging of wrong, we can't be old-school.

The other day while watching television, I came across a boxing match. I usually don't watch boxing, but for some reason I paused. The fight was just beginning. As I watched the two fighters, I could see that they were sizing each other up. One of them would hold his hands high in front of his face and shuffle toward his opponent. The other one had his hands down and was dancing all over the place. One would advance, and the other would retreat. They would shuffle and retreat. At the end of the first three-minute round, the commentator noted that he would have to judge the first round a draw. It had to be a draw, because one fighter threw one punch, and the other fighter threw two, with neither causing any damage. It didn't take me long to turn the fight off. For one thing, I really do not like boxing, and for the second, they were not doing what they were trained to do. There was no action. Sometimes I think the world sees Christians in that same manner. They look at us; they give us a moment. Even though they really do not like Christianity and they seldom think of God, every once in a while they pause. And if they do not see any action, if they do not see us fulfilling the words of Jesus, they quickly turn away and move on.

AVENGING OF WRONG: I WILL CLEAR MY NAME

The last stage of repentance is the action stage. The process of repentance leads to an intellectual aspect, an emotional aspect, and now the volitional aspect. For repentance to bear the full fruit of obedience, it is imperative that we act.

James teaches us that pointed truth in his letter: "But prove yourselves doers of the word, and not merely hearers who delude themselves" (James 1:22).

He follows this with an extended passage which deals with faith and works. It is very important to note that James is not saying that works are a substitute for faith. He is saying that the focus of our works should be to reflect the love of God. We can never work our way into God's favor. We can express our great love for God and our faith in God by doing what he wants us to do.

Read this passage. Another word for works is *action*.

"What use is it, my brethren, if a man says he has faith, but he has no works [actions]? Can that faith save him? If a brother or sister is without clothing and in need of daily food, and one of you says to them, 'Go in peace, be warmed and be filled,' and yet you do not give them what is necessary for their body, what use is that? Even so faith, if it has no works [actions], is dead, being by itself. But someone may well say, 'You have faith, and I have works [actions]; show me your faith without the works [actions], and I will show you my faith by my works [actions].' You believe that God is one. You do well; the demons also believe, and shudder. But are you willing to recognize, you foolish fellow, that faith without works [actions] is useless? Was not Abraham our father justified by works [actions], when he offered up Isaac his son on the altar? You see that faith was working with his works [actions], and as a result of the works [actions], faith was perfected; and the Scripture was fulfilled which says, 'And Abraham believed God, and it was reckoned to him as righteousness,' and he was called the friend of God. You see that a man is justified by works [actions], and not by faith alone. And in the same way was not Rahab the harlot also justified by works [actions], when she received the messengers and sent them out by another way? For just as the body without the spirit is dead, so also faith without works [actions] is dead" (James 2:14–26).

The world sees our actions.

Would you surmise that a person was happy if they never smiled?

Would you surmise that a person was physically fit if they never exercised?

Would you surmise that a person was supporting a candidate for office if they did not vote?

Would you surmise that a person really wanted to be well if they did not take their prescribed medicine?

Would you surmise that a person was really repentant if they never acted on God's teaching of how to achieve repentance?

After the conclusion of a session on restoration at a men's retreat in San Antonio, this elderly man approached me and wanted to talk. He told me that he had a son who was an agnostic. He had tried to witness to him, but his son really did not want anything to do with what his father was telling him. And because of that difference, there developed a strain in the relationship. During the session, I talked about taking action to restore relationships. As this elderly gentleman shared with me the difficulty of his relationship with his son, he made this statement, "I'm old-school. I talked to him, and if he wants to talk to me, he can call." When it comes to avenging of wrong, we can't be old-school. God has called us to take the first step, to approach those we have wronged, and to act in his name.

Why should we act? Remember Acts 3:19? "Repent therefore and return, that your sins may be wiped away, in order that times of refreshing may come from the presence of the Lord."

We must act so that the times of refreshing may come from the presence of the Lord. Doing it God's way makes a great difference. This is what one college student wrote following a conference on repentance:

"My name is Amanda, and I attended your lecture at 'Honest To God' about purifying your heart. I promised myself that I would e-mail you to let you know how things went. I had been struggling with a sin in my life that I had confessed to God, truly hated myself for, repented, and thought that was enough. Little did I know that when you sin against another person, God also wants you to make it right with them. Not only did my sin cause the other person to sin, but I'm sure that that person will never see Christians the same way again, all because of me. (Can you tell that I am still struggling with guilt?) Your lecture taught me that sometimes our sin doesn't stop at confession and repentance. I approached the person, apologized, and explained that what I did was very wrong, not like me, and I didn't know what I was thinking at the time. I can't even begin to explain the difference that has made in my life. Thank you. Thank you not only for being a disciple of Christ and teaching about him, but for being obedient to him also. Thank you."

When Amanda acted, she received the reward. She experienced a great time of refreshing.

We must act and be obedient to what our Lord tells us to do. Scripture makes this clear:

"And why do you call Me, 'Lord, Lord,' and do not do what I say?" (Luke 6:46).

"But prove yourselves doers of the word, and not merely hearers who delude themselve." (James 1:22).

"Therefore everyone who hears these words of Mine, and acts upon them, may be compared to a wise man, who built his house upon the rock. And the rain descended, and the floods came, and the winds blew, and burst against that house; and yet it did not fall, for it had been founded upon the rock. And everyone who hears these words of Mine, and does not act upon them, will be like a foolish man, who built his house upon the sand. And the rain descended, and the floods came, and the winds blew, and burst against that house; and it fell, and great was its fall" (Matthew 7:24–27).

Jesus knew the key to our being obedient. He knew that we must act, and that the action must reflect the rock-solid teaching of his Father's truth. One of the clearest mandates we have from Jesus is, "As you are going, make disciples!" We can talk about it all we want to. We can define what a disciple is. We can be trained in disciple-making. But until we engage someone with the truths of God's word, we are not making disciples. Knowledge is preparation. The power is in the application.

Growing up in a small town in north central Texas, I did not have any exposure to snow skiing except what I saw on TV. One spring, I was part of a mission trip that went to work among Native Americans in Santa Fe, New Mexico. After a few days, we had a break, and some in our group wanted to go snow skiing. I didn't go the first day because I had only brought tennis shoes, and I thought that you had to supply boots for the skies to attach to. (I told you I came from a small town in Texas). When the group returned that evening, they told me that you could rent boots and skies. The next day I went. I didn't have the money to take lessons, so I watched others. I then strapped on the skies and down the hill I went. Not knowing how to stop, turn, or even stand up made for a very long day. It was one of the most miserable days of my life—I was too proud to stop and too inexperienced for control. After that adventure, I filed snow skiing on my list of things never to do again. But in a couple of years, I had another opportunity. This time I took lessons. Instructors helped me apply good technique. And it wasn't long before the applied knowledge provided greater freedom.

Some of us have filed Christian action on our list of things never to do again. We seem to have a lot of knowledge about what we think a Christian should do and how one should be blessed. But our lives seem to be restricted. Where is the freedom? Where is the blessing? Where is the joy, the peace, and the love? They are not there because we have learned the truths but not applied them. We have a good metal picture of what we think it should be like, but we have not allowed God to work through us. We have been just been content for God to work in us.

"For behold what earnestness this very thing, this godly sorrow, has produced in you: what vindication of yourselves, what indignation, what fear, what longing, what zeal, what avenging of wrong! In everything you demonstrated yourselves to be innocent in the matter" (II Corinthians 7:11).

The pertinent question to ask at this point is, "How can I avenge what I did wrong?

To avenge what is wrong is to see justice done. You are sitting in judgment of yourself. You, through the power of the Holy Spirit, identify what you did wrong, and you adjudicate the appropriate action to make sure that justice is done.

Here are some ideas concerning restitution which will help you accomplish that goal:

If it is a mental sin, keep it mental. Picture a revival service. The preacher is pouring on the motivation to repent. His desire is to see God move in a mighty way. He wants everyone to take responsibility for their sins and then take the necessary actions to find forgiveness and release.

He pounds the pulpit and yells, "If you have sinned against anyone, go to that person and ask forgiveness! If you have thought bad things about someone, go to that person, confess, and ask for forgiveness! Judgment is to begin with the house of God, so we must be clean. During our invitation, I ask you to act on what the Holy Spirit is telling. Now is the time!"

As the invitation progresses, people begin to move. A person leaves the pew you are on and goes to embrace someone across the way. And then someone taps on your shoulder. It is a friend. "For a long time, I have held a grudge against you. You always seem to think that you are better than others. Well, I want you to know that I need to ask for your forgiveness." Of course, you embrace your friend and say you will forgive. Tears are shed. At the close of the service on your way to the car, you begin to wonder how long she had held that grudge. And Satan begins his work. You ponder, "I wonder what other things she thought about me?" And instead of sensing a release, you feel bound by a confession that you had no idea was coming.

If you have a problem with someone and the problem has remained in your thoughts, then seek forgiveness and restoration with God, not with the person. It is so easy for Satan to put things into our minds. What happens in your mind is between you and God. The complete process of repentance is a war held on the battlefield of your mind. The goal is to allow God to win and for you to surrender to his cleansing process.

"Let the wicked forsake his way, and the unrighteous man his thoughts; and let him return to the Lord, And He will have compassion on him; and to our God, for He will abundantly pardon" (Isaiah 55:7).

When we act wickedly, we are to forsake our thoughts. We are to abandon them. We are to cast them upon Jesus. He cares deeply for us and wants us to find freedom.

"For the word of God is living and active and sharper than any two-edged sword, and piercing as far as the division of soul and spirit, of both joints and marrow, and able to judge the thoughts and intentions of the heart" (Hebrews 4:12).

It is God who judges our thoughts. He knows all of them. He doesn't expect us to reveal our every thought. We can commit sin in our hearts, and in our hearts is where we need to find God's forgiveness.

If you think someone has something against you, go to them. Have you blown it and tried to forget it? You know that you treated someone in an ungodly manner, and you just let it lie, hoping that it would go away. But the Holy Spirit makes sure that it doesn't.

Have you ever gotten the feeling that there is something wrong between you and another person? They have not said anything about it that you know of, but there is a tension.

Have you ever had a person approach you and tell you that another person is mad at you?

How do you handle that?

"If therefore you are presenting your offering at the altar, and there remember that your brother has something against you, leave your offering there before the altar, and go your way; first be reconciled to your brother, and then come and present your offering" (Matthew 5:23–24).

If we even think that someone has something against us, we are to approach them and seek reconciliation. We are called to be peacemakers. Almost all of Paul's letters begin with him wishing his readers grace and peace. God offers us grace so that we can be graceful to others. He gives us peace so that we can be peacemakers. Do what makes for peace and what helps people feel the power of grace.

Approach them with humility. You might say, "I sense that there is something not quite right between us. Is there something that I have done that has caused you pain? I really want our relationship to be healthy. Maybe I am wrong with the way I am thinking, but I want you to know that I value you."

Or you may know that this person has said something to someone else about you. You approach and say, "It has been brought to my attention that there might be a problem between us. I really would like for our relationship to be restored. Would you please share with me your concerns? I would like for there to be peace between us."

And when you are the one who has caused the problem, and the Holy Spirit keeps working on you, go to the person, admit your sin, and ask for forgiveness.

Please do not go blaming the other person involved. Don't go with a self-righteousness attitude. Don't go trying to justify your feelings or actions. You are seeking peace, not seeking to establish how righteous you are. You are seeking reconciliation, not retaliation.

If the sin is public, seek forgiveness publicly. There are times when we will sin. We will talk about someone or we will pass on gossip that we cannot substantiate. We will even try to assassinate someone's character. We can get very mean-spirited. When the Holy Spirit convicts us of our sin, part of the repentance process is restoration. If you have talked about someone to others in an ungodly way, you must go to the people who heard your sin and ask for forgiveness. You must then seek out the one you talked about and ask for forgiveness. You made it public, so you must deal with it in public.

A very good general guideline for seeking restoration is found in the program *Celebrate Recovery*. In the section entitled, "Eight Principles Based on the Beatitudes" by Pastor Rick Warren, number six reads this way: "Evaluate all my relationships. Offer forgiveness to those who have hurt me and make amends for harm I've done to others, except when to do so would harm them or others."

We must go with no expectations as to how the person will respond. Reconciliation is two-sided. Our goal is for the relationship to be restored. Sometimes that will not happen. The party we approach will want nothing to do with us or our intention.

This is where you focus on God. This is where you judge God's thoughts of yourself much more highly than another person's thoughts about you.

Do you know about the relationship that David had with King Saul? David was anointed by Samuel as the next king of Israel. This was during the reign of King Saul. And because David sought the heart of God, he would not raise a hand against King Saul, who was also anointed by God. There were many times when David could have killed Saul and destroyed the threat on his own life. He would spare King Saul and cry out to him. In I Samuel 24:8–22, we have one such incident: "Now afterward David arose and went out of the cave and called after Saul, saying, 'My lord the king!' And when Saul looked behind him, David bowed with his face to the ground and prostrated himself. And David said to Saul, 'Why do you listen to the words of men, saying, "Behold, David seeks to harm you"? Behold, this day your eyes have seen that the Lord had given you today into my hand in the cave, and some said to kill you, but my eye had pity on you; and I said, "I will not stretch out my hand against my lord, for he is the Lord's anointed." Now, my father, see! Indeed, see the edge of your robe in my hand! For in that I cut off the edge of your robe and did not kill you, know and perceive that there is no evil or rebellion in my hands, and I have not sinned against you, though you are lying in wait for my life to take it. May the Lord judge between you and me, and may the Lord avenge me on you; but my hand shall not be against you. As the proverb of the ancients says, "Out of the wicked comes forth wickedness;"

but my hand shall not be against you. After whom has the king of Israel come out? Whom are you pursuing? A dead dog, a single flea? The Lord therefore be judge and decide between you and me; and may He see and plead my cause, and deliver me from your hand.' Now it came about when David had finished speaking these words to Saul, that Saul said, 'Is this your voice, my son David?' Then Saul lifted up his voice and wept. And he said to David, 'You are more righteous than I; for you have dealt well with me, while I have dealt wickedly with you. And you have declared today that you have done good to me, that the Lord delivered me into your hand and yet you did not kill me. For if a man finds his enemy, will he let him go away safely? May the Lord therefore reward you with good in return for what you have done to me this day. And now, behold, I know that you shall surely be king, and that the kingdom of Israel shall be established in your hand. So now swear to me by the Lord that you will not cut off my descendants after me, and that you will not destroy my name from my father's household.' And David swore to Saul. And Saul went to his home, but David and his men went up to the stronghold."

It would have been wonderful if the animosity would have stopped there. But it did not. King Saul spoke words of reconciliation, but it wasn't very long until Saul sent an army of 3,000 men to kill David. King Saul spoke words of peace, but he quickly forgot what he had said.

You are going to find that there will be those who will speak the words of peace, but they also quickly forget, and they will do everything they can to assassinate your character. It is in those times that we must depend upon God to protect us—just as he protected David from his greatest enemy.

Give grace. The young man died from a gunshot wound to the chest. This was his mother's baby boy. The sorrow was so heavy that she had trouble breathing. The grief was so deep. He was her only child. He was the one she was going to look to in her old age. With her husband having abandoned her long ago, there was little hope on the horizon.

The promise of her Savior to never leave her nor forsake her never meant more. She was walking in the valley of death. As she read her Bible for strength, she would cringe every time she was prodded to forgive. How could she forgive? How could she forgive the one who had taken her boy away?

The more she cried out to God, the more she was convicted. She knew she must forgive. And forgive she did. She went to the prison. She requested a meeting. And in that, meeting she told her son's killer that she had forgiven him. It was a gift of grace.

Sometimes the avenging of wrong comes from the victim. It is the victim giving grace to the perpetrator. It is giving something to someone who doesn't deserve it. Just like Jesus did for us. Jesus loved us. Jesus died for us. And still we betrayed him. But he still loves us. How hard this is. This act is so Christ-like.

Jesus believes in us. God trusts us to carry out his work. We fail. We quit. We refuse. But he still gives us a chance to do his will. Sometimes we have to put ourselves in a vulnerable position, trusting in a person who has let us down. Could we not act like our Lord and give the gift of a new beginning?

When you have done all you can, move on. Oswald Chambers writes these words: "In the Garden of Gethsemane, the disciples went to sleep when they should have stayed awake, and once they realized what they had done, it produced despair. The sense of having done something irreversible tends to make us despair. We say, 'Well, it's all over and ruined now, what's the point in trying anymore?'

If we think this kind of despair is an exception, we are mistaken. It is a very ordinary human experience. Whenever we realize we have not taken advantage of a magnificent opportunity, we are apt to sink into despair. But Jesus comes and lovingly says to us, in essence, 'Sleep on now. That opportunity is lost forever, and you can't change that. But get up, and let's go on to the next thing.' In other words, let the past sleep, but let it sleep in the sweet embrace of Christ, and let us go on into the invincible future with Him."

There will be experiences like this in each of our lives. We will have times of despair caused by real events in our lives, and we will be unable to lift ourselves out of them. The disciples, in this instance, had done a downright unthinkable thing—they had gone to sleep instead of watching with Jesus. But our Lord came to them, taking the spiritual initiative against their despair, and said, in effect, "Get up, and do the next thing." If we are inspired by God, what is the next thing? It is to trust him absolutely and to pray on the basis of his redemption.

Never let your past failures defeat your next step.

When you have done everything that you are commanded to do, you must turn it over to Jesus. We are to cast all our cares upon him, because he cares deeply for us.

Rita Springer sings a song that will help someone move on. Read the words below:

"I want the joy of the Lord to come down
I want the joy of the Lord to fall now
I want the joy of the Lord in my life
I want the joy of the Lord to lift me
I want the joy of the Lord to change me
I want the joy of the Lord in my life.
"It's time I started dancing over all these graves
It's time I gave you all my God the highest praise

It's time to lift my voice and beg for this blessing to fall.

"I want the joy of the Lord to come down
I want the joy of the Lord to fall now
I want the joy of the Lord in my life
I wan the joy of the Lord to lift me
I want the joy of the Lord to change me
I want the joy of the Lord in my life.

"It's time I started dancing over all these graves
It's time I gave you all my God the highest praise
It's time to lift my voice and come on we got to beg for this blessing to fall."

We all have graves in our lives. There are things that have died, and there is no way to resurrect them. You have done all that it is possible to do. We can't let the failures of the past keep us from moving on. There are times when the only thing we have is God's grace. Accept it, and keep moving toward God. Get out of the graveyard and on the highway to recovery.

Maintain the pliability of your heart. The Spirit of God moves in us as we open up passageways. Obstructions arise where there is sin. Unconfessed sin is like sandbags of the soul which retard the flow of the living water of life. An unrepentant heart is like a shriveled sponge gasping for that living water. Our hearts can grow hard.

If you will constantly practice four simple principles, you will be able to maintain the pliability of your heart:

1. Receive forgiveness
2. Ask for forgiveness
3. Give forgiveness
4. Seek forgiveness

Receive forgiveness: "If we confess our sins, He is faithful and righteous to forgive us our sins and to cleanse us from all unrighteousness" (I John 1:9). God will offer, and you must think yourself worthy of receiving it.

Ask for forgiveness: When you are wrong, or when there is a break in the relationship that is caused by or aided by your sin, ask for forgiveness. Ask God to forgive you, and then ask those involved to forgive you.

Give forgiveness: If we forgive, we will be forgiven. If we do not, then we will not be forgiven. It is so much better to give forgiveness so you can have forgiveness.

Seek forgiveness: Take the initiative. When the Holy Spirit convicts you of sin, take immediate steps to deal with it.

God gave me this poem many years ago. It is simple, but the message brings hope:

"Today is a new beginning; it is the present not the past.
What people have said about me hopefully won't last.
Today is a new dawning but even it will go out
But then this new beginning will be what they talk about."

When we focus on obedience, when we believe in the message of repentance, and when we act based on God's revealed truth, we will experience times of refreshing. The living water of the gospel will flow through us and restore the vibrancy of our life!

Now is the time to act.

I would like to help in any way I can, and I would like to hear the ways God uses the truths in this book. Please feel free to e-mail me at edwright22@gmail.com.

LaVergne, TN USA
24 June 2010
187266LV00001B/1/P